FAMILY

INTERVENTION

Ending the cycle of addiction and co-dependency

by Frank L. Picard, M.S.

Published by:
Beyond Words Publishing, Inc.
Pumpkin Ridge Road
Route 3, Box 492-B
Hillsboro, OR 97123
Phone: 1-503-647-5109
Toll Free: 1-800-284-9673

The information contained in this book is intended to be
educational and not for diagnosis, prescription, or treatment
of disease or of any health disorder whatsoever. This information should not replace competent professional treatment
or medical care. The contents of the book are intended to
be used as an adjunct to a rational and responsible drug and
alcohol care program prescribed by a treatment professional
or doctor. The author and publisher are in no way liable for
any use or misuse of the material.

The case studies in this book are real; however,
the names, circumstances and locations have been
substantially changed to protect the anonymity
and confidentiality of all cases.

Printed in the United States of America by Arcata Graphics,
Kingsport, Tennessee

ISBN: 0-941-831-38-8
Library of Congress Catalog Card Number: 89-061-264

Cover design by Rob Pawlak

Dedication

To my brothers, David and Roland.
Each died as a result of the disease and dysfunction
before they had an opportunity
to find the internal peace that I have found,
but they are at eternal peace.

About the Author

After recovery from his own addiction to alcohol in 1976, Frank Picard began a rigorous course of study to complete his undergraduate degree. He subsequently received a master's degree in psychology through the Department of Alcohol Studies at Washington State University.

Since the completion of his degree work in 1979, Mr. Picard has spent the majority of his time in private practice in Portland, Oregon. He has become widely recognized as an expert in the field of intervention, as well as on issues concerning adult children of alcoholics. He has successfully guided over 1,000 interventions in 26 states and in Canada, and has written several articles on intervention and adult children's issues. *Family Intervention* is his first book.

Numerous organizations, including major corporations, colleges, universities, hospitals, and churches, have relied on Mr. Picard's expertise in the area of addictions and adult children's issues. He is frequently called upon to provide workshops and training in the areas of intervention, adult children, and the dysfunctional family.

Mr. Picard may be reached at 1-800-344-1827.

Table of Contents

*This chapter provides readers with criteria for evaluating
whether the people they care about have a disease that will not
allow them to seek help on their own. It outlines the three stages
of chemical dependency and indicates that, barring a major
crisis, the addictive process will progress in a continued
downward spiral.*

*In spite of the fact that intervention has been around and
accepted for years, the general public's view is that it is
confrontational. The fear of confrontation keeps families
from moving forward with intervention. This chapter begins
to ease the readers' fears of the intervention process. It
describes why confrontation fails, then begins to lay the
groundwork for successful family intervention.*

*This chapter further removes the fears that the family feels about
intervention. It describes the dual personality of the alcoholic/
chemically dependent person and outlines safe and loving ways
to reach that person in such a way that he or she will accept
treatment. This chapter will rekindle hope.*

Acknowledgments

When undertaking a work such as this it is difficult to know whom to thank, and especially how not to leave out people who contributed in a major way to its development. I have concluded that it is impossible to acknowledge all those who played major or minor roles. There are, however, certain individuals and institutions without whose guidance, mentoring, and acceptance this work would not have been possible.

The first on that list has to be the Heartview Foundation in Mandan, North Dakota. Heartview is one of the finest inpatient facilities for treatment of the disease of chemical dependency. It is the place that gave me hope in 1976. The people there not only gave me hope; they also helped me to believe in myself, to realize that I have value. That is where my spiritual awakening occurred and where my journey began. But it was only a beginning. Because I grew up in a highly dysfunctional home, much more healing was necessary. It is with a deep sense of gratitude that I thank the therapists who worked with me on ACOA (Adult Children of Alcoholics) issues long before that term was fashionable. To Russ, Al, Ray, Keith — each of you in your own way helped me to succeed and to learn how not to sabotage myself.

Next are the thousand families who over the years have entrusted me with their interventions. From each of you, as families and as individuals, I have learned a great deal. From the very first interventions that were done in milking parlors and wheat fields in North Dakota to the interventions that occurred in the board rooms of major corporations, all of you have taught me that each intervention, each alcoholic and each family is the same even while each individual, each family and each situation is unique. Your trust and your gentle teaching are gratefully acknowledged.

I would also like to acknowledge interventionists generally around the country who, for the most part, perform the most important and difficult task there is in this field. The most difficult aspect of treatment of the disease of chemical dependency is getting patients to acknowledge their need. So for those of you who have been doing interventions in silence and with minimal recognition, know that your contribution is immense.

Finally, I offer special thanks to my family. My sons, Jim and Bob, provided much support. Their "You can do it, Dad" attitude has helped keep me going. The unwavering support, patience, encouragement and loyalty of my wife, Pat, have been a source of strength. Her patience with Mac, the computer, as she transcribed this work and her patience with me as I struggled to stick with the task of writing make a mere thank-you seem quite inadequate.

Introduction

The theory that addiction to alcohol and other mood-altering substances is a disease has long been accepted by the medical and psychiatric establishments. Nevertheless, we as a society still want to believe that solving the problems of addiction is as simple as "just saying no." As a professional who has long dealt with addiction, I see little evidence that either the general public or the addiction profession itself regards alcohol and drug abuse as a disease.

Perhaps because health problems so often involve subtleties and intricacies not readily apparent to untrained eyes, public attitudes tend to ignore and avoid these complexities. But like the proverbial ostrich with its head in the sand, our culture depends on a one-dimensional, simplistic view of alcoholism and drug addiction that places us all at great risk.

Not only are we as a society failing to make headway in solving this problem; we are actually losing ground. The rate of increase in alcoholics and drug addicts is reaching what may be catastrophic levels. Moreover, addicts are not the only ones who are affected by this disease. Each addict directly affects the lives of the family members and friends who are close to him. These people also suffer lasting damage.

We are at a crossroads. We must come to grips with this disease and the toll it is taking on our people. Unless we can turn the corner in the next several years and begin reducing the number of alcoholics and addicts — and consequently the number of lives that are affected indirectly by addiction — we will have done irreparable damage to the fabric of our culture. The multi-generational dysfunction that this epidemic will leave us with includes adults and young people who are handicapped by their own compulsive disorders, unable to bond, unable to form committed relationships, unable to experience personal success. This crisis is truly at the eleventh hour. It is not too late to reverse the trend, but simplistic answers and slogans will no longer suffice.

In an attempt to help the addict deal with his problem, the addict's family members and other loved ones often become involved in a process which we call "intervention." During this procedure, the most important people in the addict's life try to break through his denial that he has a problem and that he needs help. Depending on how intervention is handled, it can either succeed in opening the door to treatment or can hinder the very recovery that it is meant to effect. How family members can contribute to a successful intervention is the subject of this book.

The concept of intervention is not new; its origin goes back to the founding of Alcoholics Anonymous in the 1930s. In 1980, Dr. Vernon Johnson's book *I'll Quit Tomorrow* clarified the concept of intervention and emphasized its importance in the treatment process.

Unfortunately, since then many people have come to accept the view that with a little bit of knowledge, family members can "intervene on" their loved ones without professional guidance. But expecting family members to handle their own interventions in the complex disease of addiction is like expecting relatives to operate on loved ones who need surgery. More often than we would like to admit, the result is not intervention but rather a confrontation that further fractures the family system. If we are indeed dealing with a disease, then it is unrealistic to expect family members to be able to diagnose and interrupt the disease's process on their own. If I may borrow from the familiar adage, a little knowledge about intervention can be a dangerous thing.

This is a book about intervention, not confrontation. By explaining the complexities involved in intervention, this book can help the reader understand that simplistic approaches are not the answer. But most of all, this is a book about hope: hope for the alcoholic; hope for the drug addict; hope especially for family members, because they will realize that they no longer need to assess, diagnose, and begin the treatment process on their own.

Professionally guided intervention, in the hands of a trained practitioner who understands the subtleties and intricacies of this disease, is successful 95 percent of the time. The more than a thousand successful interventions that I have had the privilege of guiding have taught me that intervention is not something separate from treatment, but rather is the first step in treatment. How intervention is handled not only affects the outcome of treatment, but also the extent to which the entire family is healed. This book is intended to help you to find the hope needed to initiate the recovery process which so many families have successfully undertaken.

Though the material in this book speaks most directly to the family member of the chemically dependent person, it has been reviewed extensively by friends and colleagues in the treatment profession. Experts who had relied on confrontation as part of their day-to-day work with alcoholics, addicts and their families have highly endorsed this work, each in his or her own way. Having something to offer other than confrontation, they report, has improved their counseling skills. I could not have hoped for more.

1

Addiction: The Deadly Disease

While medical technology is advancing at an almost exponential pace, the disease of addiction remains vastly misunderstood, misdiagnosed, and mistreated. As a culture we are very quick to be filled with disdain for the drug addict. Cocaine, heroin, acid, and marijuana are readily identifiable as drugs, and no one disputes that they are harmful and addictive. Alcohol, however, is another matter.

In our culture today we are far more inclined to see alcohol as a beverage, not as the powerful drug that it is. Alcohol is a drug, and alcoholism is an addiction to it. Our society's acceptance of nicotine as an addictive drug is far more widespread than our recognition and acceptance of alcohol as a drug, as evidenced by the amount of attention given by the Surgeon General and others to health-warning labels on products containing nicotine. Yet the side effects of alcohol are pervasive and extremely damaging.

Research tells us that as little as a few ounces of alcohol can cause irreparable damage to the fetus during pregnancy. A few

1

ounces of alcohol in an adult affects motor skills and impairs vision as well as hearing. Though research has provided us with much evidence about alcohol's addictive properties, we as a culture want to protect our belief that it is a beverage rather than a drug. Actors like Dean Martin and Foster Brooks fill our concert halls and auditoriums with comedy performances about the effects of alcohol; we are far more inclined to laugh at its effects than to be saddened by its destructive powers.

Medical research on alcoholism has identified multiple stages of the disease, from its very early onset to delirium tremens and death. But in spite of that research our society is still far more inclined to think of alcoholics as those who are on skid row and who suffer from DTs. Those who reach this stage are but a very small percentage of the alcoholics in our country. The rest die long before the disease has progressed that far.

The purpose of this book is not to debate whether or not alcoholism is a disease, nor to debate whether or not alcohol is a drug. Both are widely recognized and accepted facts among professionals. We as a culture, however, still lag far behind.

For a drug to be addictive, three properties must be present:

1. It affects mood.
2. It affects the central nervous system.
3. The organism develops a tolerance to the drug.

Alcohol scores well on all three counts. Initially it acts as a euphorant and lifts the mood of the consumer; then it acts as a sedative. It dramatically affects the central nervous system, causing the impairment of motor control, speech, hearing, and vision. And tolerance is identifiable simply by observing that with increased drinking experience an individual is able to handle more and more alcohol and outwardly show less effect.

In my practice I have developed the following criteria which can help you assess your own particular situation and can aid in your determination of whether or not you or your loved ones are suffering from the disease of alcoholism:

1. Hereditary factors
2. Loss of control
3. Failure to learn from experience

Though these criteria are not completely exhaustive, they provide a framework in which to evaluate your situation.

Hereditary Factors

The research of Goodwin, Lieber and many others leaves no doubt that there is a genetic predisposition toward alcoholism. The genetic link is well established and is no longer debated. In over a dozen years of experience with addictions, I have been unable to document a single case in which we were able to rule out hereditary factors. When families first look at this criterion, frequently their initial response is that no one they know of was an alcoholic. We must keep in mind that in looking at family history it is extremely rare to find the sort of definitive diagnosis that can only come about from treatment. Treatment has only been in existence for a few decades. Alcoholism has been accepted as a disease for just over thirty years. Alcoholism has been listed as a cause of death on death certificates for an even shorter period of time.

To help determine hereditary factors I encourage you to look at the private discourse within the family. If you examine the patterns of conversation within a family with an alcohol problem

you will probably hear the alcoholic referred to only by innu-
endo in statements like:

> "Well, he always drank."
> "He could hold his liquor."
> "Rarely did he ever get out of control."
> "He was a real boozer."

Rather than seeking records of a specific diagnosis of alcoholism, look for the innuendos and the observations and reports of
behavior.

It is not uncommon to find that such a family includes a generation of teetotalers. Those who have extreme views about the
consumption of alcohol generally have a history of very negative and painful experiences with alcohol while they were
growing up. Also, it often happens that alcoholics are more or
less excommunicated from their families. Look for siblings of
the parents or grandparents whom you rarely heard about and
never visited and who seemed almost nonexistent. Often the
family member who is estranged or separated from the family
is the alcoholic no one wants to talk about.

Don't be afraid to ask questions about your family tree. However, I caution you not to use the label alcoholic when making
this inquiry. Ask about family members' drinking patterns and
behavior rather than whether Uncle Louie was an alcoholic.
Since for many the diagnosis of alcoholism means the presence
of delirium tremens, asking whether or not Uncle Louie was an
alcoholic will probably bring a negative response. If you can,
ask about how much he drank:

> How frequently did he drink?
> Were people worried about his drinking?
> Did it cause him any problems?

Do you remember him trying to stop or control his drinking?

This type of inquiry into your family history is more apt to give you information on which to base your own assessment. Asking about alcoholics will frequently bring a one-word negative response.

The offspring of alcoholics have at least an even chance of becoming alcoholics if they start using alcohol. If hereditary factors are present on both sides of the family, the odds of developing this disease are even greater.

Loss of Control

The second criterion that I use to facilitate an understanding and acceptance of the disease of alcoholism is loss of control. Anyone who uses the drug alcohol to any extent is at some point in time going to have some negative experiences as a result of that usage. When an individual makes specific plans about how much he or she is going to drink on a particular occasion and then loses the ability to stick to those plans, that individual is experiencing a loss of control. An example of this would be a person who plans to stop for a beer after work and get home for dinner by seven, but who ends up drinking much more than just that one beer and being driven home at two in the morning. This loss of control rarely occurs each time an alcoholic drinks, but rather on a random and unpredictable basis.

When you are using this particular criterion to evaluate your own personal situation or that of your loved one, I encourage you to pay very little attention to the frequency with which a person drinks or the amount of alcohol consumed. Rather, pay attention to his or her words, and pay particular attention to results. Because of the negative consequences of drinking alcohol, an individual who continues to drink makes very specific plans to prevent the reoccurrence of such consequences. Listen to people's words as they announce to you the adjustments they will make to prevent the same difficulties from reoccurring.

No person can experience a blackout without feeling a great deal of concern. No person can experience an arrest for driving under the influence without being alarmed. No person can see the pain in his or her spouse's or children's faces the next day without feeling remorse. As a result, such individuals will publicly or privately attempt to make a commitment to limit their consumption of alcohol to a lower level. If they are already well on the way to developing the disease, the failure of these plans will be accompanied by rationalizations and justifications; the addict will claim that each lapse was an exception due to special circumstances. As loved ones we are more inclined to pay attention to and believe these rationalizations and justifications than we are to look at specific behaviors and subsequent results.

There is a type of alcoholism in which the individual simply plans on a repeated basis to get intoxicated. However, that type is fairly rare, and is indicative of the late stage of alcoholism. During the early and middle stages, individuals frequently plan the opposite:

> They plan to drink, not to cause problems.
> They plan to be sociable, not to ruin the party.
> They plan to have fun, not to be argumentative.
> They plan to feel good, not to get sick.

Alcoholics by nature are kind, caring, and sensitive people. They do not intentionally set out to inflict emotional pain on their loved ones. Listen to the plans they make concerning their drinking, in terms of both amount and frequency as well as behavior, and observe the results. If on an intermittent or nearly continual basis the resultant alcohol consumption exceeds the plan, chances are that your loved one has a drinking problem. Loss of control has very little to do with the amount a person drinks or with the frequency of drinking. It has to do with results.

Failure to Learn from Experience

The third factor that I utilize in my practice to help bring about an understanding and an acceptance of this disease is the failure to learn from experience. Because alcoholics are kind, sensitive and caring, they are emotionally affected by the negative results of their drinking behavior. In the early stages of this disease they will express guilt, remorse and regret as a result of the problems that have occurred while they were drinking. The human capacity to learn and the sophistication of that learning separate humans from other animals. Physical and emotional pain are powerful teachers and motivators of change. Early on the alcoholic will experience considerable emotional pain as a result of his or her drinking behavior and will verbalize that pain. The guilt that the alcoholic feels, coupled with remorse, results in promises to cut down, control or quit drinking. These promises are heartfelt and sincere, but they are not often kept.

To help understand this particular category better, let us look at a specific example. A year or so ago, in preparing for an intervention, a 16-year-old girl recounted a situation that went something like this. She was a star on her high school basketball team and very much enjoyed her parents' attendance at the games. However, in her junior season her father frequently showed up at the games intoxicated; throughout the game she could hear his voice in the stands over and above everyone else's, and she was continually embarrassed by his behavior. At one point his harassment of the referees and his frequent foul language brought her to tears in the locker room. She and her teammates made it to the state tournament and progressed to the finals. Prior to the championship game she sat down with her father and had a heart-to-heart talk about his drinking and behavior at the games, and the effects it was having on her. She said, "Dad, I am embarrassed by how you act, by how loud you are, and by your language." She told him about how she had cried in the locker room, about her coach's comments, and about the support her teammates had given her. She told her father how important this particular game was and how she wanted to be able to concentrate on her game, not to be constantly wondering whether he was going to be inappropriate again. Her father felt the emotional pain that his daughter was in, and felt his own pain. He promised himself and his daughter that he would not drink before the game and that she did not have anything to worry about. Their heart-to-heart talk was so profound that both of them cried and embraced and expressed their love for one another. But when the night of the championship game came, there was Dad in the stands again, loud, vulgar and intoxicated. Dad had lost the ability to learn from experience and to learn from the most powerful teacher of all: pain. This story is not at all unique.

The repetition of negative experiences in spite of best efforts and intentions is a powerful indicator of the presence of alcoholism. What it indicates is that, at least on occasion, the alcohol is in control and not the drinker. If the drinker were in control, he or she would have stuck to plans and kept commitments. Certainly alcoholics will attempt to rationalize and justify their behavior in order to make some sense out of what seems senseless, but it will be a vain attempt to relieve some guilt and remorse. Rationalization is a normal and natural defense mechanism that comes into play. I encourage you, however, not to get caught up in the rationalizations, but to listen to the commitments that were made and observe the results.

If in reviewing your particular situation or that of your loved one you are able to identify any of the three criteria described above, then you can safely conclude that treatment and intervention are essential. However, for some it is difficult to get away from the old idea that to be alcoholic you have to drink huge quantities on a daily basis. If you have reviewed the criteria and remain unconvinced that alcohol is a problem for you or your loved one, it can be helpful to look at the situation from another angle.

One way to gain greater understanding of this disease is to look at the importance that the addict places in his or her relationship with the drug itself. We only protect and defend what is important to us. When people constantly find ways to protect their right to drink and their time to drink, then their relationship with alcohol has taken on an abnormal level of importance. If a person's actions indicate that his or her relationship with alcohol has a higher priority than relationships with spouse, children, friends or employer, that person has a serious drinking problem. In the case of our 16-year-old basketball star, her father's relationship with alcohol became more important to him than his relationship with her.

An individual who receives a driving-under-the- influence citation and then begins to drink and drive again is risking personal freedom to protect his or her relationship with alcohol. In most jurisdictions today a second conviction results in mandatory jail time. When people are willing to take that risk and all of the ramifications that go with it, including increased insurance costs, possible loss of ability to get to and from work and subsequently to be gainfully employed, and public and private humiliation, this indicates very clearly that their relationship with alcohol has reached unhealthy proportions. If alcohol causes an individual to be willing to take repeated risks with health, employment, personal relationships, or freedom, he or she is indeed alcoholic, irrespective of the frequency with which this occurs.

Because the alcoholic has been stereotyped, the words alcoholic and alcoholism trigger a great deal of fear in both alcoholics and their loved ones, and as a result a host of defense mechanisms almost immediately come to the fore. Because of the stereotypes and the resultant fear, both alcoholics and their loved ones quickly begin trying to rationalize and justify the alcoholic's behavior. When those rationalizations and justifications begin to fail on either an internal or external basis, silence occurs:

> What was talked about during the early stages of this disease now becomes a family secret.
> We protect the alcoholics from children, from employers, from their extended families, and from themselves.
> We try to control situations and circumstances, even the amount drunk.
> Most of all, we stop talking.

We stop talking about what's happening and what the results are, and the conspiracy of silence contributes to the disease. When our efforts at control fail we begin to doubt our belief in ourselves and our belief that a problem exists. The denial of the family becomes as strong as the denial of the alcoholic if left unchecked.

Being an alcoholic family has been likened to having an elephant in your living room. Everyone walks around it. Everyone pretends that they don't see it. And certainly everyone pretends that the elephant does not have an odor. The difficulty with having an elephant in the living room is that when a stranger walks into the house, he or she immediately sees the elephant and readily identifies it. The infrequent visitor will say, "Hey, this looks like an elephant." And you as a family will quickly deny that there is an elephant in your living room; you cannot for the life of you understand what is being seen or referred to. If the alcoholic is to be successfully treated, intervention must take place before the denial system of the family weaves such an entangled web that elephants are no longer visible.

The Harmful Relationship

For those who get trapped in a progressive dependency on mood-altering drugs, a powerful relationship with the drugs develops. It is this relationship that becomes most difficult for the family to understand and accept. For the person who is developing a dependent relationship on alcohol or other drugs, there is a continuous increase in the importance of that relationship. Needs are met which the addict is unable to meet in any other way. A powerful bond is created.

For the chemically dependent husband who used to think of how nice it was to be on the way home to see his partner and enjoy a relaxing evening with his family, thoughts shift from the joy of seeing his family to the joy of the first drink, to how nice it will be to get home and to have that first beer or wine or martini. After a while he begins to believe that the first, second or third drink can pick him up, make him feel relaxed, make him feel OK, better than anything else ever has.

Alcoholics long for an embrace, but not an embrace of loved ones. They long to embrace a glass, to hear the sounds of ice cubes and feel the relief that comes from that first consumption of their drug of choice. Those trapped in the web of addiction are having in essence a socially acceptable affair. When they are down, their relationship picks them up; when they are unable to relax, their relationship helps them relax; when they are unable to sleep, it helps them sleep. For those persons harmfully involved with chemicals, that first use of the mood-altering substance creates a warm feeling and sensation over their entire body. No marital, family or employer relationship can provide that.

If you as a spouse or as a family member of a chemically dependent person feel as if you are playing second fiddle to the chemical, then there is a good chance that you are. To help you evaluate whether or not the person you are concerned about has developed a harmful relationship with chemicals, ask yourself what kinds of risks this individual is willing to take to protect his or her relationship with the chemicals.

If the individual is repeatedly driving under the influence, then it follows that he or she is willing to risk safety and potentially freedom to protect the relationship with the chemical. If to protect one's relationship with a substance one is willing to risk life and limb as well as loss of freedom, the relationship has become pathological. If an individual is willing to drive while intoxicated with his family in the vehicle, his relationship with the chemical has reached the point where he is willing to risk the safety of his loved ones to protect his relationship with alcohol.

Another area of risk-taking behavior involves the alcoholic's relationship with his or her physician. When people lie to their physicians about the amount of alcohol they consume, or when their physicians raise serious health concerns related to their involvement with alcohol but they continue to drink, those individuals are placing their health and life at risk to protect their addiction.

The extent of an alcoholic's abnormal risk-taking behavior only determines the stage of the disease. The fact that this behavior is present, even on an intermittent basis, is enough to indicate that the person is an alcoholic.

Though the addict places less value on relationships with spouse and family and at times may endanger them with risk-taking behavior, this does not mean that he or she no longer loves them. What it does indicate is impairment, and that on a daily basis the family will continue to move to a position of less importance in the addict's life while the importance of the chemical increases. This happens because the addict needs the chemical, not because he or she wants it.

Robert and Mary McAuliffe have developed a tool for diagnosis that centers around the importance of the drug relationship. In their book *The Essentials for the Diagnosis of Chemical Dependency,* they define psychological dependence as "an irrational need, caused by a person's committed drug relationship, to rely on the ingestion of mood-altering chemicals in expectation of achieving rewarding psycho-physical experiences, or more concretely, in order to achieve welcome changes of feelings, moods and mind."[1] The following questions can help you to assess the situation further.

1. How prominent is the presence of alcohol or drugs?
2. Does its presence appear secretive or pronounced?

---

[1] McAuliffe, Robert and Mary, *Essentials for the Diagnosis of Chemical Dependency, Volume 2* (Minneapolis: The American Chemical Dependency Society, 1975), p. 18.

3. Does the individual find ways to consume alcohol or other chemicals in an isolated or solitary way?

4. Does the individual seem to manipulate circumstances and create opportunities to participate in events where known consumption will be occurring?

5. Is the individual avoiding health warning labels and drinking in spite of being advised not to use alcohol as medication?

6. Is there a personality change that occurs with the ingestion of chemicals?

7. Is there a mood change that occurs?

8. Does it appear that the individual manipulates lifestyles or relationships with significant others to make continued use possible?

9. Is there repeated intoxication?

10. Has interest in other activities and pursuits diminished as the level of consumption has increased?

11. When the time of the individual's first drink has been delayed, does he or she appear to be uneasy, restless, or agitated?

12. Does the individual become hostile if, for whatever reason, that delay or obstruction of the normal drinking time is increased?

13. Often you will be able to observe a pattern of rapid ingestion of the first couple of drinks. Is this occurring?

14. If you love someone who is harmfully involved with alcohol or drugs, have you at times felt:
    Frustrated?
    Angry?
    Rejected?
    Confused?
    Frightened?

Worried?

Replaced?

Ignored?

Second-class?

Discounted?

Or a host of many other most unpleasant
     feelings?

15. In response to the situation, have you:

Adjusted?

Cajoled?

Pleaded?

Begged?

Forgiven?

Promised?

Readjusted?

Blamed yourself?

Blamed others?

Ignored?

Pretended?

Covered up?

Lied?

Threatened?

Prayed?

Or made a host of other responses normal for
     a loved one of a chemically dependent
     person?

If all of this sounds way too familiar, then the chances are that you are involved with someone dependent on alcohol or other drugs. I encourage you to stop trying to understand this rationally, because you are dealing with an irrational dependence and relationship. Commit yourself to seeking help so that you can assist in the disruption of the harmful drug relationship and be a party to healing rather than enabling it to continue.

A True Disease

Practitioners of medicine long ago accepted the fact that alcoholism was a disease. They were able to do this because it had identifiable symptoms, an identifiable progression, an identifiable treatment and, if left untreated, a predictable progression towards death. For purposes of diagnosis the progression has been divided into these stages:

> Early or prodomal phase
> Middle or crucial stage
> Late or chronic stage

The following symptoms are visible in the early or prodomal stage of the disease:

> Occasional relief drinking
> The first blackout
> Occasional sneaking of drinks
> An increase in tolerance, i.e., the ability to handle more
>   alcohol before the effects show
> Gulping of the first drink
> An urgency about the first drink
> Feelings of guilt
> Drinking to relieve stress or anxiety
> Avoidance of discussion of drinking

The middle or crucial stage of the disease is characterized by these symptoms:

> Drinking accompanied by excuses
> A show of remorse
> Increased grandiosity
> Increase in blackouts
> Increase in promises and resolutions followed by
>   increased failure in carrying them out
> Loss of interest in others

Changing of friends
Changing of family habits
Change in drinking pattern
Attempts to stop drinking
Drinking earlier in the day, especially on weekends
Change of jobs, change of residence
Social engagements missed or cancelled
Absence or tardiness at work

The chronic or late stage of the disease carries these symptoms:

Decrease in tolerance
Physical deterioration
Flushed face, broken blood vessels in the nose
Elevated liver enzymes
Moral deterioration
Drinking with inferiors
Change in drinking locations to inferior taverns
First bender
Onset of lengthy periods of intoxication
Impaired thinking
Loss of job
Vague spiritual desires
Morning tremors
Obsession with drinking
Ineffectiveness of alibis, excuses and rationalizations
Permanent brain damage
Permanent insanity or death

Historically, it was the belief of professionals in the treatment field and the medical community, as well as of society at large, that nothing could be done for the alcoholic until he or she hit bottom. But, as you can see from the preceding list, the symptoms of the late stage of alcoholism include permanent brain damage, permanent insanity and death. If we wait until people hit bottom before intervening, then only a small percentage of those affected with this disease will be helped; hitting bottom is, for the most part, terminal.

The disease of addiction is no different from any other disease. Any disease is more treatable if treament is begun at an early stage. Early treatment is easier and less costly, and it has a higher success rate. The same is true for the disease of addiction. If treatment begins earlier, it tends to be more successful because there is less denial present; the patient is less defensive and more amenable to treatment. In addition, the patient has suffered less physical damage. Unfortunately, today many still want to wait until the patient is terminally ill before calling the ambulance.

Alcohol is our oldest drug and still the most popular. However, in the United States we believe that if a little is good then more has to be better. As a result we have developed significant problems with alcohol and drugs in our culture. And today, for the most part, anyone entering treatment facilities under the age of 35 is addicted to more than one substance at a time. Let's review those other substances and the symptomatology surrounding them.

Cocaine

Cocaine is not new, nor is its use. It is known to have been used centuries ago by Latin American Indians, who chewed the leaf of the coca plant as part of their religious ceremonies. Sigmund Freud reportedly experimented with cocaine, and there are those who say that he did far more than experiment. Medically, cocaine is occasionally used for certain types of nasal and oral surgeries. Primarily, however, it is an illegal street drug.

Once an infrequently used substance, cocaine gradually increased in usage until it became the drug of choice of the rich and eventually achieved its current mass popularity. In spite of the well-publicized deaths of people like John Belushi, Lenny Bias and others, its popularity has not waned. In his book *800-Cocaine,* Dr. Mark Gold states that there are 5,000 new first-time users of cocaine per day in the United States. That adds up to 150,000 first-time users per month, and nearly two million per year.

Cocaine is extremely addicting. Initial use causes a tremendous rush of euphoria, immediately banishes fatigue, removes hunger, and causes increased sexual arousal and a sense of omnipotence. This initial experience can be so powerful that some are addicted from the very first time they experiment with the drug. Because it is impossible to know how pure the cocaine is or what substances were used to decrease the purity of the cocaine, death can result upon first usage. *There is no such thing as safe recreational use of cocaine.*

Though cocaine is no longer limited to the upper class and the financially independent, it remains a relatively expensive drug; many of those who are addicted to cocaine cannot afford to be. Thus it is common for cocaine addicts to become cocaine dealers in order to help cover the cost of addiction. The moral deterioration that occurs in the cocaine addict is far more significant than it is in the alcoholic. Users go from despising dealers to being dealers, from despising addicts to being addicts. Because cocaine has a psychosexual effect, they frequently get themselves involved in sexual activity which was not previously a part of their repertoire. Because they are involved with a drug they cannot afford, often they steal from their family or pawn items of special value to themselves or their family. As the addiction progresses and behavior deteriorates, the risks that individuals take increase. They place themselves in dangerous situations and become secretive, paranoid, and protective.

One of the more difficult aspects for families to comprehend about cocaine addiction is the strength of the bond between the addict and the dealer. The cocaine addict literally elevates his supplier to the status of a god. The addict believes that the dealer can do no wrong, that the dealer is his best friend, that the dealer is one of the only people who really cares about him. The addict will defend and protect the dealer, lie for him, cover up for him, and often will enter treatment only if there is an agreement that he doesn't have to say anything about his dealer.

You as a family member or friend may not see all of the hidden side effects of cocaine addiction, but generally you will be able to observe:

1. Financial irregularities and difficulties
2. Attitude and behavioral changes
3. Extreme changes in sleeping habits such as staying up all night and sleeping long hours during the day
4. Nosebleeds
5. Sore throat
6. Sniffles
7. Sinus problems
8. Rubbing of nose
9. Decreased interest in personal health and hygiene
10. Phone callers who leave no messages
11. Phone calls at odd hours
12. Change in peer group
13. Paranoia characterized by irrational fears
14. Irritability
15. Compulsive behaviors like tapping or jiggling of feet, hair combing, tie straightening, buttoning or unbuttoning
16. Increased use of alcohol or another drug
17. Unexplained absences

18. Cash withdrawals from the bank of $25, $50 or $100
19. Lying about finances

Rarely do you see people abusing cocaine on a regular basis without there also being a pattern of increased abuse of another drug. The most frequent drug of choice for the cocaine addict to abuse simultaneously is alcohol. However, marijuana abuse is also quite prevalent. Because of the dual abuse and dual dependence, the strategy of intervention must often be quite complex.

As the abuse and addiction increases, symptoms become progressively worse. Paranoid thoughts can eventually become delusions, including auditory, visual, olfactory and tactile hallucinations. Addicts may have an awareness that their paranoid symptoms are not real and have enough self-control not to act on them, but they will remain hypervigilant, constantly checking their environment. This makes the addict extremely unpredictable.

It is important to remember these major facts regarding cocaine:

1. It is highly addictive.
2. It is extremely dangerous, and major psychiatric and physical problems, including death, can occur from the initial usage.
3. Addiction progresses rapidly.
4. Intervention is difficult.
5. Prognosis is poor.

Marijuana

Perhaps no drug today is shrouded in more misinformation than marijuana. There are still many who believe it is a nonaddictive drug and that it is not harmful. Neither belief is correct. If you recall, we stated that a drug is addictive if it meets the following criteria:

1. It affects mood.
2. It affects the central nervous system.
3. The organism develops a tolerance to the drug.

Like alcohol and cocaine, all three criteria are met by marijuana. Because its active ingredient, THC, is stored in fatty tissue, much of it remains in brain tissue for a prolonged period of time. As a result of its absorption into brain tissue, it affects the following functions:

1. Comprehension
2. Memory
3. Sleep
4. Emotions
5. Coordination
6. Vision
7. Blood pressure
8. Heart rate
9. Brain waves

Since the organs of the reproductive system contain a high percentage of fatty tissue, marijuana also has an adverse effect on the testosterone level in both men and women, decreasing it in males and increasing it in females. It reduces the number of sperm and may even alter the chromosomes of reproductive cells, thereby creating birth defects in offspring. If marijuana is used during pregnancy there is an increase in the mortality rate and in the number of birth defects. In addition, THC is passed to babies through breast milk. Clearly marijuana is not only addictive, but also highly dangerous. If you are concerned about a loved one's potential marijuana abuse, look for the following symptoms:

1. A change from active participation in family life to passive withdrawal, not only from the family but from normal interests
2. A decline in the quality of performance on the job or at school
3. An alienation from family and friends and a lack of consideration for the feelings and ideas of others
4. Chronic or frequent redness of the eyes
5. A decline in personal hygiene
6. An increased level of defensiveness when mild restrictions are experienced or observations are offered
7. Neglect of family responsibilities
8. A change in weight
9. Unexplained secretive phone calls
10. A change in peer group

The marijuana that is available today on the streets has a THC content that is anywhere from 3 to 16 times greater than the THC content in the marijuana that was available in the 1960s. Because the marijuana grower is generally more concerned with making money than with the health of others, the varieties of marijuana grown today are often treated with pesticides, causing even greater toxicity and more unpredictable results and side effects. These are the important facts to remember about marijuana:

1. Its potency is much higher than it used to be.
2. It is highly addictive.
3. It causes physical damage, and the damage is greatest in the body systems that contain fatty tissue.
4. It is a drug that is rarely used alone; generally the individual is simultaneously using another substance.
5. Recovery from the addiction is slow.
6. It takes years to regain normal brain function and alertness.

7. Its use is illegal, and addicts are often involved in other illegal activities, including dealing.

Other Addictive Substances

There are many other abused drugs besides alcohol, cocaine, and marijuana. The degree of use of these drugs varies considerably, depending on location. In the inner cities the use and abuse of street-manufactured methamphetamine, a highly dangerous drug that is snorted or used intravenously, is increasing at an alarming rate. Additionally, the use of acids such as LSD and Angel Dust are on the increase again in some areas.

In addition to the street drugs, there is a wide variety of pharmaceutical preparations that are abused and highly addictive. All of the major and minor tranquilizers have addictive properties. Narcotics and synthetic narcotic pain relievers are addictive and very frequently abused. Prescription drugs such as valium are also used frequently in conjunction with alcohol. Watch for the following signs if you are concerned about your loved one being harmfully involved with prescription drugs:

1. Ignoring health warning labels regarding the use of alcohol
2. Finishing the prescription before the normal time
3. Calling the doctor for refills
4. Seeing more than one physician and receiving similar prescriptions from all of them

The combination of alcohol and prescription drugs can be deadly. Often a drink plus a pill can have four to eight times the effect of one pill or drink alone.

Worksheets

Here are some worksheets to help you accept and understand whether or not a problem exists.

1. What evidence is there of a genetic link?

   Parents

   Grandparents

   Aunts

   Uncles

2. What evidence is there of a loss of control?

   Cite times when the outcome was different from the plan.

Cite commitments made that were sincere but not kept.

Cite examples of failure to learn from painful experiences.

2

The Development of Intervention

Just as there is much mythology and misunderstanding among the public about the disease of chemical dependency, the practice of intervention is also poorly understood. Although intervention in various forms has been practiced for many years, its application has not been as frequent or as effective as it might be.

The first discussions of alcoholism as a disease and advocacy of intervention began in the early 1930s, when Alcoholics Anonymous was founded. One of the founders, "Bill W." (Bill Wilson), made numerous visits to late-stage alcoholics in jails and hospitals to bring a message of hope. In his visits Bill W. was able to share with them the symptoms of their disease and the pain it was causing them, and he offered an alternative to that pain. Though his approach was unstructured, Bill W. was the first person to regularly put into practice the idea that we do not need to wait until the alcoholic or chemically dependent person comes to us to ask for help; the right thing to do is to go to them. (In spite of his view, many of the people in Alcoholics

Anonymous support groups object to intervention on the grounds that it doesn't allow people to "hit bottom.")

The pioneer of structured intervention was Dr. Vernon Johnson of the Johnson Institute. He has described his work in two books, *I'll Quit Tomorrow* (1980) and *Intervention* (1986). Dr. Johnson's premise is very simple. It is that alcoholism is a disease that has identifiable symptoms of both a physical and an emotional nature and that the disease progresses in a continued downward spiral. If the disease is uninterrupted, the affected individual will ultimately deteriorate both mentally and physicially. The end result is death. Dr. Johnson saw that our culture's belief that we need to allow the chemically dependent person to "hit bottom" was insane. He knew we had to reach the alcoholic and chemically dependent person before that point was reached.

Dr. Johnson's pioneering work has made an immense contribution to this field. Although my views on intervention are not in agreement with his views on every point, I hold nothing but the highest respect and regard for Dr. Johnson and his contributions to the suffering alcoholic and addict.

To understand intervention theory and how it has evolved, it is important to view its foundation. In *I'll Quit Tomorrow*, Dr. Johnson described a typical scene from an early type of family intervention. The family of an alcoholic physician had consulted a counselor to learn about the disease and how to intervene. All of the family members were asked to make a list of specific behaviors of the alcoholic father and husband that were causing them concern. Then they met with the alcoholic on their own. This was the scene as described by Dr. Johnson:

> The meeting was called at the doctor's office in a building he owned. It was his afternoon off, and he was alone. The young clergyman

came directly to the point: "Actually, we are here to talk to you, Dad, about our deep concern with what is happening. Since it is no doubt going to be painful, I'm going to start out by asking you to promise, please, to hear us out." His goal was to create the father's role as a listener and then to keep him in that role.

The father was furious. His eyes were blazing. He leapt to his feet and paced the floor. "If you think I'm going to listen to all that again, you've got another think coming!" It was a tirade.

Gently, throughout the demonstration, the son persisted, "Sit down, Dad, sit down, please!" Finally, the father sat down and fairly shouted, "All right! I know what you're going to say, but go ahead and say it if it'll make you feel any better!"

The daughter reached into her pocket, pulled out a written list, and began timorously and fearfully. "Dad, I came home from school last Thursday with two girlfriends. We came in the front door making so much noise that we woke you up on the couch. You swore at my friends so, Dad, that I'm ashamed ever to bring them over again, but I think you were so drunk that you can't remember that!"

This enraged him. He jumped to his feet and put his face six inches from hers. "After all I have done for you," he shouted, "you dare talk to me like that!" The daughter burst into tears.

The young clergyman intervened. "Dad, Dad, please hear us out! Please!" Finally he quieted his father and asked his sister to continue. She went on with more such events, just as specific as the first, while he pretended not to listen.

Finally, he had to drop that pretense and started pushing her along. "That's twenty," he would interrupt her, as she started a new incident. "What's twenty-one?" This crazy game went on. Finally she was through.

The twenty-year-old son was next, and in a voice that trembled a bit he began quietly, "Dad, I know what you probably will do to me, but gosh, I've been worried to death, so I've got to tell it like it is. I'm your janitor in this building, and I cleaned it thoroughly three weeks ago. A week later I found five empty Scotch bottles in the places I had cleaned the week before. You're drinking on the job, Dad!" The father tried to wipe him out with a glare, but remained silent. The young man continued through the descriptions of four or five equally specific incidents that had caused him concern. When he finished, the father's tone was menacing. "I'll take care of you, all right!" he said.

The wife was next, and she was so fearful of his reaction that she apologized at length for what she was about to do. "I supose this is the end of us, but then I'm convinced it would be anyway." But she plunged in. "What really got me scared happened two weeks ago," she said, and then related the story of a summons he had received on a charge of assault with a deadly weapon. "He has a gun permit because of the narcotics in his bag. And in a drunken moment, he waved his pistol in the wrong face and is being sued."

At that point, the other three in the room all exclaimed, "Mom, we didn't know that! When did that happen?" She turned to the two of her children who had already spoken and said, "I didn't know most of the things you just told about either."

She continued with her list, and a few episodes later the father jumped to his feet and dashed from the room. The family sat in stunned silence. While they were wondering what to do next, back he came carrying a case of scotch whiskey which he put at his wife's feet, exclaiming heatedly, "Okay! Okay! I get the point! You take that and get rid of it. I quit drinking!"

She was greatly relieved and obviously ready to stop, but the older son sat his father down gently, over loud protestations, and urged his mother on. Bewildered, she continued, and a few minutes later the father jumped up and disappeared again. This time he returned with four partly filled bottles, obviously from various hiding places. Again he placed them at his wife's feet. "You take those too. Now I do quit!"

She waited until he sat down again and went on reading from her list. She came to one of the last items. "Last Tuesday," she said, "there was an emergency phone call for you. I had to say the doctor was out, and you were, too, on the couch. There was no way you could have answered that emergency, being as heavily under the influence as you were."

During the recounting of this incident, his whole demeanor changed. All the belligerence just melted away. His hands went over his face, with his elbows on his knees. It was clear that he was quietly crying.

"The patient died," his wife went on, "and I know what that cost you. I know your devotion to your patients over the last twenty-five years. I know your commitment to the Hippocratic Oath. I know what that cost you." And she was finished.

The doctor went on quietly crying, but all of a sudden something hit him as he realized there was still one person in the room left to speak. This was almost the most poignant moment of all. He lowered his hands and looked at his clergyman son and shook his head as if to say, "You don't have to say anything." The respect and love they had for each other was apparent during this silent interchange.

The son nodded back at him, then broke the silence gently. "Yes, I do, Dad. I'm the one who arranged this afternoon."[1]

Though the process was difficult for this physician's family, the family was successful and their loved one did enter treatment. By lovingly confronting the alcoholic with the reality of the disease symptoms, they were able to initiate the recovery process.

The use of Dr. Johnson's basic model of intervention has had an 80% rate of success at the Johnson Institute. However, for many this method of intervention appears to be so scary and difficult that they are too afraid to try it. Today, advances in the field of intervention have made it possible to avoid the shouting matches which are characteristic of the old intervention method.

Dr. Johnson's work has had three important benefits. First, it helped to destroy the myth that alcoholics and addicts will not

---

[1] Johnson, Vern, *I'll Quit Tomorrow* (New York: Harper & Row, 1980), pp. 51-3.

change until they "hit bottom." Second, it was empowering; it gave families a sense of hope that they could make a difference. Third, his pioneering efforts became the foundation for the work in the field of intervention that was to follow. Because of Dr. Johnson, hundreds of thousands of alcoholics and addicts are alive today.

There are seven basic guiding principles in Dr. Johnson's style of intervention, as outlined in *I'll Quit Tomorrow.*

1. Facts should be presented by significant persons in the addict's life.
2. These persons should describe specific events which have occurred or conditions which exist.
3. The tone of the confrontation should not be judgmental. Instead, interveners should show genuine respect and concern as they confront the addict with the truth of his or her situation.
4. Whenever possible, the evidence should be linked directly to the drinking or drug-using.
5. The evidence should be presented in explicit detail to give the addict a clear overall view of his or her behavior during a given period of time.
6. The purpose of the presentation of this material is to have the alcoholic see and accept enough reality about his condition so that, however grudgingly, he or she will accept help.
7. When that goal is achieved, the available choices acceptable to the interveners may be offered. For example: "Do you wish treatment center A or B?"

Each of these seven points is essential to the intervention process. However I have some specific concerns about Dr. Johnson's model of intervention:

1. An objective professional is not present.
2. It is far too scary for some families.
3. It is confrontational in nature.
4. Ultimatums are often needed.
5. Anger frequently results.

During the history and development of intervention, the words intervention and confrontation have frequently been used interchangeably. I believe they are two distinct concepts. It does not take therapeutic skill to confront; it does to intervene. Confrontation is not new to alcoholic families, and in fact they may have confronted the alcoholic many times before considering intervention. As a result of that history, they are often reluctant to attempt to confront the alcoholic again because they do not want to meet with failure once more. Nor do they want to have to deal with the anger that generally results from confrontations. Even the word confrontation tends to elicit feelings of fear, anxiety and hurt. From the very outset of the intervention process it is best to eliminate this word from the vocabulary.

Families who do their own confrontations make the tacit assumption that they are healthy and objective. They hope that at least one person in the family will remain detached enough to prevent the confrontation from deteriorating. But this assumption is often incorrect. The disease of chemical dependency is a family disease. Each member of the family and each person close to the alcoholic or drug addict is affected and infected by the same disease. Each family member needs treatment as much as the chemically dependent person (except for the need for detox), and each has developed his or her own denial system and false belief system.

To clarify why I believe that a family on its own lacks the objectivity to do an intervention, let us look at the dysfunctional roles that develop within a typical chemically dependent family system. In this section I have drawn on the work of Sharon Wegscheider-Cruse, Virginia Satir, Claudia Black and others who have written extensively about the roles that develop within chemically dependent families.

The Chief Enabler. In the alcoholic and chemically dependent family the Chief Enabler serves an extremely important role. Chief Enablers work tirelessly and endlessly to keep the family system together. They continually take on increased responsibility for the health and welfare of the family, such as the managing of finances and other tasks that had been done jointly. They keep secrets about the addict's behavior from the children or from the extended family, and they apologize and cover up for that behavior. They work hard to keep things running smoothly, to not ruffle any feathers, and to avoid family conflicts or disagreements that the alcoholic or chemically dependent person might use as an excuse to drink or to take drugs. They act as a shock absorber for the chemically dependent person. When the addict is about to experience consequences of his or her disease, the Chief Enabler tries to block or to cushion the blow.

Chief Enablers are the people closest to the alcoholic or addict. They scurry the children to their rooms so the children won't see dad or mom intoxicated. They cancel social engagements so that friends or members of the extended family do not see the impairment. They manufacture excuses for behaviors. The progression of this enabling runs parallel to the progression of the disease. The more advanced the disease is, the more the Chief Enabler loses objectivity and strengthens his or her own defense mechanisms.

The Family Hero. Another of the identifiable roles in the chemically dependent family system is that of the Family Hero. Often this is the oldest child. This individual works extremely hard; he or she is the straight-A student, the athlete, the one active in drama or debate, the one who receives academic and professional recognition. Frequently the Family Hero is also the family therapist. Attempting to console and comfort the Enabler, he or she becomes the Enabler's confidant. The Enabler and others outside the family system often reinforce the Family Hero in this role with such statements as, "I don't know what this family would do without you." Family Heroes play very necessary roles in dysfunctional families. Their achievements and their successes help provide some badly needed self-esteem to the family as a whole.

Outwardly the Family Hero looks like a model person, but inwardly he or she feels lonely, lost, hurt, and angry. In addition, he or she feels torn between loyalty to the chemically dependent person and loyalty to the Enabler. Often Family Heroes initiate the intervention. But again, because of the role is they have been forced to play in their sick family systems, Family Heroes lack the objectivity to intervene on their own.

The Lost Child. This individual deals with the stress and turmoil caused by alcoholism and chemical dependency by slowly but steadily withdrawing into isolation. This is the child who spends time in his or her room alone, with few friends and only solitary activities. The Lost Child has learned to deal with the intermittent or continuous crises in the household by swallowing feelings, isolating, and withdrawing. These unhealthy coping mechanisms result from a fear of conflict and confrontation.

The Family Mascot. I enjoy listening to comedians. I am struck by the number of comics whose routines consist of jokes about the family. I wonder how many grew up in dysfunctional families and learned to use humor to cope. Family Mascots are the ones in the family system who can find ways to laugh in moments of crisis and chaos. They use humor to relieve their own stress, anxiety and fear. They also attempt to take care of the other members of the family by helping them to laugh at what is occurring. At the same time as humor serves to cover up the Mascot's own true feelings of pain and hurt, it also helps the family to avoid dealing with the pain within the family system. The person playing this role lacks the objectivity necessary to undertake self-run interventions. Interventions are very stressful; often the Family Mascot will make jokes at crucial points, thus unknowingly sabotaging the process.

The Scapegoat. The Scapegoat is that individual who frequently takes the blame for the family's dysfunction and "takes the heat off" the chemically dependent person. The so-called black sheep of the family acts out the family dysfunction, trying in a subconscious way to call attention to the sick family system. In adolescence, those in this role may get involved in drugs, teenage pregnancy and multiple acts of delinquency. They are the individuals who get in the most trouble at school. Their role is essential to the dysfuntional family system because it provides a major excuse for the behavior of the alcoholic or chemically dependent person. Often the Chief Enabler and the Family Hero also depend upon the person in this role to serve as Scapegoat.

I know of no knowledgeable professional in the field of mental health or addictions who does not believe that these various roles within the family system develop and that the entire family system becomes affected and infected by the disease of addiction. If trained professionals now agree about this concept of the dysfunctional family sytem, then how can we expect families to be objective enough to do interventions on their own? Each individual within the family system needs guidance and support from a trained professional for intervention to be therapeutic.

Without that professional guidance, the likelihood is great that defense mechanisms and unhealthy coping skills will surface during the intervention and cause it to fail. The end result is more family pain, more scapegoating and blaming, a further fracturing of the family system, and a forcing of the family into an even deeper well of secrecy.

Even when a self-guided confrontation is successful and the prospective patient does enter treatment, serious problems may arise. Oftentimes the patient will enter treatment with so much anger that the first several days of treatment will be wasted in terms of any therapeutic benefit. The anger generated through the confrontation may take months to heal, and may cause family members a great deal of fear and heightened anxiety. The family may be left wondering whether or not they did the right thing.

A professionally trained interventionist working with the family system throughout the pre-intervention, the intervention itself and the post-intervention can prevent these problems from occurring. In addition, a professionally guided intervention by a properly trained clinician will take into account the disease and dysfunction of the entire family system. Rather than asking the families to overcome their defense mechanisms and dysfunction to confront the chemically dependent person on their own, the clinician will work with those defense mechanisms to help the families intervene rather than confront. Professionally trained interventionists can also help by:

> lowering the threshold of fear
> encouraging a sense of safety
> providing support
> supplying much needed objectivity

> assisting each participant to move from a
> dysfunctional role to a role which involves
> healthier communication

The Family Secret and Family Shame. Another reason that it is wise to seek professional help for intervention is to break the pattern of family secrets and family shame. No one person in the family system knows all of what is happening. Each person knows a little bit, but no one talks openly and honestly about what is occurring. Each member of the alcoholic or chemically dependent family system feels a sense of guilt and shame and is afraid to let anyone else know. In fact, each feels the same sense of guilt and shame that the alcoholic or chemically dependent person feels.

Going outside the family system for professional help breaks the family rule of secrecy and says that what has happened is not going to be hidden anymore. That act empowers the family to a considerable degree. It also gives the chemically dependent person or alcoholic permission to accept help in a way that does not often occur with self-run interventions, which tend to reinforce the secret. Having a professional present makes it easier for family members to say, "If everyone knows, I may as well face it."

Though confrontation can be very powerful and can elicit the results the family is looking for, it also can be frightening and risks aggravating the worst part of the disease both for the addict and for the family. If we truly intervene rather than confront, the power for change comes from love and from the heart and these negative effects are avoided.

3

Understanding Chemical Dependency

Those close to the chemically dependent person find it very difficult to understand and accept the changes occurring within that person. The often erratic nature of those changes makes them not only confusing, but easy to interpret as a lack of love and commitment.

However, it is possible to understand the belief system and personality that evolves with the disease of chemical dependency. The more you can comprehend this belief system and personality, the more objective you will be about the disease. When you are able to see that the behavior changes of the person you are close to are not aimed at you, when you can avoid taking them personally, you will be able to intervene much more successfully.

The A and B Sides of the Personality

In order to understand the chemically dependent person in your life, it is helpful to think of his or her personality as having two sides: A and B. A represents the behaviors which the person has developed as defense mechanisms; B is the basic core personality — what the person's nature is when not in the grip of the disease of chemical dependency.

A = The defense mechanisms developed by the chemically dependent

B = Core personality and beliefs

The B Side. Chemically dependent people, by their very nature, are kind, sensitive, big-hearted, altruistic, loving, gentle and caring. It is this core structure of their personality that makes coming to grips with the disease so very difficult both for them and for those close to them. They are the people who will go out of their way to help someone in need. They are the people who will find the most ways of saying "I love you." As the disease progresses, this kind, sensitive side of the person becomes more and more difficult to see as it becomes progressively obscured by defense mechanisms.

The A Side. The A side of the personality structure of the chemically dependent person is where the defense mechanisms of the dependency are found. The chemically dependent person will deny, rationalize, justify, defend and blame. And when all the other defenses fail, anger will surface and the person will simply tell you to mind your own damn business: "This is my life. What I do is up to me. You take care of you and I'll take care of me."

The extent to which these defense mechanisms are present depends solely on the stage that the individual's disease of dependency has reached. The more advanced the disease, the more these defense mechanisms and behavior will dominate the core personality. The defense mechanisms evolve to protect the psyche of the affected individual. They are there to help protect that individual from feeling the overwhelming sense of guilt and shame that would come with facing the behavior and the symptoms of this disease head on. Defense mechanisms are neither good nor bad, but natural: difficult to understand and to cope with, but not bad.

A dictionary of psychological terminology defines a defense mechanism as "an involuntary or unconscious measure adopted by an individual to protect himself against the painful effect associated with some highly disagreeable situation, physical or mental, of frequent occurrence; it may be employed to cover a wide range of phenomena."[1] In other words, these mechanisms are not malicious or purposeful; they are not used deliberately to inflict emotional pain on you or other loved ones. Chemically dependent persons act and behave the way they do because they need to, not because they want to.

At this point I encourage you to get a notepad and pen and begin trying to get in touch with both sides of the person you are concerned about. With paper and pen in hand, first try to remember some of the times when the naturally kind, sensitive and caring side of that person was present; jot down some notes that will help you to recall these later on. Below I have provided a list to help jog your memory. For each item listed, try to briefly identify a time when you were aware of the B side of the chemically dependent person. Some of the items on the list may also trigger memories of the addictive side, but for now let's just stick with the core personality. What was it that this person did or said that showed the B side of the personality? Maybe it was nothing more than a look, a feeling, a touch.

---

[1] Drever, James, *A Dictionary of Psychology* (Middlesex, England: Penguin, 1952), p. 61.

Special moments in your relationship
    Dating times
    Engagement
    Wedding day
    Honeymoon
    Special intimate talks
    Times when you felt especially close
Special times as parents
    Pregnancy
    Childbirth
    Illnesses
    Special activities
    First report card
    Times when you talked about parenting, how it
        was going to be different, how it was going
        to be better
    Times you shared your hopes and dreams
        for your children
    Times with other children
Times when other people were in need
    Neighbors
    Friends
    Deaths of neighbors or friends
    Illnesses of friends, neighbors, co-workers

If you are a child of someone who is chemically dependent, attempt to get in touch with some of the times when you felt that this parent cared: Christmas, a birthday, your first bicycle, first school play, first school concert, first date, first school dance. What did this person say or do that let you know you were loved and cared for?

If you are an employer, think about the person's behavior toward other employees, and his or her acts of kindness toward those experiencing difficulty. Remember examples of a willingness to help, a willingness to go out of the way, to do extra things, and to show commitment.

If you are a friend, remember the times when your friend has spoken lovingly of his or her spouse or children, or has been of aid and assistance to you.

Remember that if the disease of dependency has progressed very far, you may only be able to see this B side of the person by looking at the past. The more progressed the disease becomes, the less visible the core personality is and the further back in your memory you will need to look. Be aware also that sometimes it is initially difficult to remember the good that is in this person because your own hurt and anger are in the way. These feelings are as normal as the defense mechanisms of the chemically dependent person! Your interventionist will help you deal with that anger, which is your defense mechanism, so that you will be able to assist in the intervention. Don't try to swallow it and pretend it isn't there, and certainly don't get angry at yourself for feeling what is normal and natural.

It is very important to the intervention process that you develop an understanding of the chemically dependent person. It is equally important that you understand how this disease has affected you, and what defense mechanisms you have developed to help cope with it. There is no way that one can be emotionally involved with a chemically dependent person without experiencing hurt. Because of the presence of the disease, the chances to deal with that hurt within the context of the relationship become infrequent and often nonexistent. The lack of such opportunity creates anger.

The environment created by the disease of chemical dependency does not allow us to deal with anger in a constructive way. Unresolved anger leads to repression, and then to denial and covering up. In fact, the closer one is to the chemically dependent person, the more susceptible one is to developing the same defense mechanisms as the chemically dependent person. For example, the spouse of the chemically dependent person can also develop the ability to rationalize, justify, defend, blame and deny.

Keeping your pen and paper handy, now begin to identify some of the times when you have seen the A side of the person you are concerned about, the defense mechanisms that are a normal and natural part of this disease. Remember that those defense mechanisms are the ability to deny, rationalize, justify, defend, blame, and minimize one's behavior. If those fail, anger and rage ensue.

As you may recall, one of the identifying characteristics of this disease is the loss of control. This is demonstrated by an individual's inability to maintain a specific plan about his or her drinking or using drugs. Try to remember the various times when the person made commitments regarding consumption of alcohol or drugs. The following list should be helpful.

    Special occasions
    Birthdays
    Anniversaries
    Having company for dinner
    Family events
    Children's events
    Vacations

What was the commitment, what happened, and what defense mechanism surfaced? How did the alcoholic or chemically dependent person rationalize, justify and defend the behavior and the consumption? What guilt, remorse and regret were expressed? What promises about next time were made? If children are involved, think of times when they felt hurt, sad, scared, or embarrassed.

Try to remember specifics for each defense mechanism we have mentioned. Following are some common excuses:

I lost track of time.
I was just visiting.
I got too busy.
It doesn't happen very often.
It was a special occasion.
It's just wine.
It's just beer.

Who or what does the alcoholic or chemically dependent person blame: a hard day at work, lots of stress, lots of tension, the kids, you, the in-laws, the boss, a coworker, "someone" who spiked the drink, the weather? Remember that we are not doing this to be judgmental; we simply are trying to pinpoint the symptoms of the disease. Think of specific instances when the chemically dependent person tried to rationalize consumption and behavior, and think of particular excuses that were used:

I just had a few.
I hadn't eaten.
I had eaten.
I ate the wrong stuff.
I was tired.

Think of times when his or her anger surfaced and:

you feared for your safety
things were broken
the children or you were abused

These exercises have probably helped you become aware that the personality of the one you are concerned about has two distinct sides. The closer you are to the person, the more progressed the disease, and the longer you have been involved, the more your objectivity will be affected. Don't let that stop you, however. Seek assistance from your interventionist. If you have been close to the person for a long time, identifying both sides of this individual may take a considerable amount of time and energy. Continue to remind yourself that you are not dealing with right and wrong or good and bad, and that what is occurring is a normal and natural part of the disease process. The more we are able to get away from subjectively placing a value judgment on what is occurring, the more able we are to intervene.

The Belief System of the Chemically Dependent Person

Besides developing certain defense mechanisms which affect their personalities, chemically dependent people also evolve an identifiable belief system. The belief system consists of four distinct components, which are:

1. The knowledge that he or she has a problem
2. The belief that others would not understand
3. The belief that he or she would be rejected if others knew the extent of the problem
4. The belief that his or her situation is unique

Let's look at each individual component of this belief system.

Knowledge of the problem. The individuals will not necessarily use the terms "alcoholic," "drug addict" or "chemically dependent" in describing themselves, but they will indirectly reveal their awareness of the problem. For example, they may acknowledge inappropriate consumption and use the terms "problem drinker" and "alcohol abuser." Those close to the chemically dependent person may not notice these indications of awareness because they are very quickly followed by excuses and rationalizations of the behavior. Nevertheless, if you think back to the early stages of the disease, you will be able to identify several times when the individual admitted that what was occurring was indeed a problem.

The average person with whom I intervene has already in some way sought help on three separate occasions. The difficulty is that these people do not seek specific help for their addiction; the untrained individuals or organizations they go to for help are unable to pick up the hints and cues that are given about the chemical dependency. Because the same belief system develops within the family, family members also will have sought help an average of three times before the intervention. The most common persons they consult for help are pastors, marriage counselors, or family physicians. In each such contact, hints and innuendos usually point to the true problem, but the untrained professional does not know how to read these cues and so is unable to assist in the way that is needed. By the time of my intervention, the alcoholic or chemically dependent person, too, already will have talked to a friend, medical doctor or counselor, and may even have called Alcoholics Anonymous or a treatment center. But each of those attempts turns into an effort on the part of the addict to prove that he or she is unique. Such attempts don't help individuals to recognize the seriousness of their problem or to request specific assistance for their alcohol or drug problem. Treatment facilities and information and referral services on alcohol and drug abuse get numerous anonymous calls from individuals wanting information about "a friend." The more the disease progresses, the more the chemically dependent person seeks information to prove that he or she does not have the disease: "I know I have a problem, but...."

"You don't understand." This component of the individual's belief system is quite sincere. In their heart of hearts the chemically dependent truly believe that others do not and would not understand. For, in fact, they themselves don't. They do not understand how they can make commitments and not follow through, how they can make plans and not stick to them, and how they can be kind, loving and sensitive one day yet be angry, belligerent and mean the next. "If I cannot understand my behavior and my lack of control, certainly others will not."

This belief is reinforced for the chemically dependent person by his or her day-to-day interactions with others. How many times have you told yourself and your loved one that you don't understand? Even when the words aren't spoken, body language and facial expressions say it very loudly. That look of bewilderment conveys a clear meaning to the chemically dependent person.

"Others will not accept me." As the disease progresses, self-esteem erodes. Many of the actions of chemically dependent people are known only to themselves. You may never have had an opportunity to observe them sneaking drinks, but they have observed themselves. As the disease progresses, their behavior becomes more and more secretive, and their self-esteem erodes. The belief that no one could accept them if they knew the full picture becomes stronger and stronger. This belief can become so dominant that suicide becomes a viable option. The disease of chemical dependency breeds self-loathing, self-disgust, self-hatred and shame.

The patterns of action and behavior that alcoholics and chemically dependent people develop are unacceptable even to themselves. That lack of self-acceptance is then projected onto others and becomes a core part of the belief system. As the disease progresses, this belief grows stronger, yet it may be outwardly demonstrated less often.

"I'm different. I'm unique." There are numerous ways in which the chemically dependent person demonstrates this aspect of the belief system. We see individuals redefining what it is that constitutes a problem. They explain why so-and-so has a problem and they don't. If they go to an AA meeting they come home armored with the differences they have noticed, not the similarities. From an evaluation, they may grasp only the symptoms they don't have rather than those they have. Another aspect of this belief is that the person is convinced that there is nothing that will help his or her particular problem: "It works for other kinds of alcoholics and addicts, but it wouldn't work for me." Remember that we are dealing with a strong genetic component in the disease of chemical dependency. This individual's image of an alcoholic or an addict may be based on a parent or relative whom they swore they would never be like. Therefore they focus on the differences between themselves and that image.

Naturally, the chemically dependent person will define a problem as something which he or she does not quite have. As the disease progresses the definition of who it is that has a problem will continue to change:

From "people who drink and drive" to "people who
  get more than one drunk-driving ticket"
From "someone who can't get home on time for dinner"
  to "someone who is out all night"
From "an individual drinking out of control on an
  intermittent basis" to "someone who is out of
  control every night"
From "someone who is out of control at home" to
  "someone whose drinking or drug usage interferes
  with work"
From "people who have drug or alcohol problems at
  work" to "people whose addiction causes severe
  physical impairment."

Continual redefinition of what constitutes a problem is quite
common. It fits very well with the rest of the belief system:
knowing that you have a problem but believing that no one
would understand or accept you, believing that the problem
you have is different and somehow unique, and therefore re-
sorting to denial and hopelessness.

The family of the alcoholic tends to develop the same belief
system. How many times have you as a loved one said, "I know
it's a problem but you don't understand"?

How many times have you sincerely felt that neighbors,
  friends, or members of the extended family really
  do not understand, that they don't understand the
  stress and the pressure that your loved one is under?
  Certainly others would not understand what goes on
  behind closed doors.
Not only would they not understand, but certainly they
  could not accept the Jekyll and Hyde personalities
  that you have seen.

> They couldn't understand or accept the sexual conflicts,
>   the extramarital affairs, the impotence.
> And besides that, the situation you deal with really is
>   different than most.
> He is not as bad as . . .
> He doesn't drink as much as . . .
> And besides that he is so good about . . .
> He's not at all like John or Mary.
> He's never missed work.
> He's never beaten me.
> He's never played around on me.

Try to get in touch with all the different ways you've tried to convince yourself and others that your situation truly is unique and different. Try to identify the different aspects of this disease that you felt others wouldn't understand or accept. Try to recognize how you have redefined what a problem is.

Just as this false belief system leads alcoholics and addicts to denial and hopelessness, the corresponding beliefs of those close to them have the same effect. Identify your own denial and hopelessness. Think of the various times you've covered up:

> Cancelling a dinner party
> Declining invitations from neighbors, friends and
>   extended family
> Making excuses for inappropriate conduct
> Giving excuses to the children
> Blaming the children

Remember the various times when you told yourself or others that if certain things happened you would take some action, and then when those things did happen you did not follow through. Each time those events occurred you found ways to rationalize and justify your inaction. "It probably won't happen again," and "Besides, he or she promised that it wouldn't happen again."

Remember that the belief system of the co-dependent is very similar to that of the chemically dependent person, though the behavior and defense mechanisms it triggers may differ. The more you can identify this belief system in yourself and develop an awareness of how it has played itself out in your day-to-day situation, the better prepared you will be to assist in intervention.

As you develop insight into how you have accepted and acted on this belief system, I caution you to avoid blaming and criticizing yourself. Though that may tend to be your initial response, know that it is as normal and natural for you to have developed these beliefs as for the chemically dependent person to have done so. Do not look upon it as your failing but as part of the disease of co-dependency or para-alcoholism. The more you are able to view it as symptomatology rather than as personal failing, the more successful you will be. You are not the true villain here and neither is the chemically dependent person. The villain is the substance and the disease. The more you understand how the disease progresses and how it has affected you, the more successful you are going to be.

4

The Intervention Process

To help you understand intervention, let me first share its essential components:

1. Bathing the chemically dependent person in love
2. Immersing that person in the reality of the problem — in words he or she can hear
3. Providing the person with viable solutions to the problem

The first, essential requirement of those who participate in intervention is that they truly care about the well-being of the addicted individual. A participant's genuine concern is vital to the success of an intervention — it is even more important than the afflicted person's full understanding of the disease. This concern needs to be expressed in a way that is not going to trigger the defense mechanisms of the chemically dependent person.

The second requirement of intervention participants is the ability to communicate reality in a way the chemically dependent person will understand. I believe that the English language can be our powerful ally or our worst enemy in the intervention process. A successful intervention depends on our choice of words and on how we express them. It is critically important that the chemically dependent person hear the reality of his or her impairment, but that reality needs to be communicated in a way that is hearable, not in a way that is going to trigger (again) the defense mechanisms of this disease. If reality is communicated in anger, it will elicit anger. If it is communicated in the form of blame, it will result in blame. If it is communicated in a way in which the behavior is justified or excused, it will elicit justification and excuses. But if it is communicated concretely, accurately, and with compassion, it has the potential to elicit change.

The third essential requirement of those who intervene is that they provide viable solutions. The only solution available for someone affected with the disease of chemical dependency is intensive treatment. Stopping the use of a chemical allows treatment to occur but it does not solve the chemical dependency problem without that treatment. The changing of jobs, relationships or locales does not solve anything either; such changes are mere coping mechanisms, coping mechanisms that will ultimately fail.

To make the treatment solution viable one needs to eliminate the excuses for avoiding treatment. If time off from work is necessary, then arrange it. If financial assistance is necessary to be able to afford treatment, then arrange it. Whatever reasons may prevent an individual from accepting treatment need to be dealt with openly and honestly so they are no longer obstacles. Then when the intervention occurs the individual will be faced with the choice of accepting a viable solution or denying the love he or she has just received. Chemically dependent people, by the very nature of their disease, do some very dumb things, but they are not stupid. If not accepting treatment no longer has any viable rationale, they will see that the treatment is practicable and they will accept it.

In general, the intervention process must neutralize the primary belief system of the chemically dependent person and avoid triggering the defense mechanisms that the disease presents.

The difference between intervention and confrontation is in the love that is shared. If that love is shared in a real, hearable way, confrontation can be avoided. I ask each participant in the intervention to write out word for word exactly what he or she is going to say so that we can get a solid grasp of the hearability of those words.

Participants should begin by stating why they came to the intervention: because they care for the chemically dependent individual. Secondly, I ask them to share why they care. What is it about this person that they find endearing? What is good and decent about this person? What is special? Then I ask them to share a few specific examples of the person's admirable traits. In other words, what is the evidence that the B side of the personality exists — that kind, sensitive, caring, altruistic side?

When a participant begins with a statement of concern for the chemically dependent person, the communication is anchored in love and concerns about the disease become more hearable. These concerns recognize the symptoms of the disease; they don't blame the individual afflicted with the chemical dependency.

Let me give you an example (names, situations and locations have been changed). In a recent intervention a woman spoke eloquently of her chemically dependent friend's behavior and support during the time of her father's death. She talked about this friend being there with her at the hospital when her father died, of all of the various chores that he took over during the time of the funeral and immediately following, and of his many kind words of support. Not only did she speak of his kind and sensitive behavior; she also spoke about what his actions meant to her personally. The data sheet she prepared for the intervention went something like this: "John, I am here today because I care about you. We have been friends for a long time and that friendship has meant a great deal to me. I think of especially those times when you've been there as a friend for me like the time last fall when my father died. You stayed with me at the hospital when Dad was dying because none of my family was able to be here. As my family began to arrive you went out of your way to extend a helping hand, to provide some housing and to show that you cared in many ways. You came over and cut my lawn and offered many words of encouragement and support. It meant a great deal to me."

The First Step: Seek Guidance

Once you as a family member or a friend of an alcoholic or chemically dependent person have become concerned about the individual's level of involvement with alcohol or other drugs, it is time to seek help. I encourage you from the outset not to prejudge or predetermine whether intervention is a viable option, but simply to seek professional guidance and assistance to help determine the level of impairment and what treatment options are available, including intervention.

Because other members of the family system may not have progressed to the same level of understanding of the problem that you have, I encourage you to be cautious in terms of whom you invite to go with you, and to consider the possibility of initially seeing a professional alone, getting guidance on who else ought to be involved besides yourself.

The purpose of the first session with a professionally trained interventionist is to allow that professional to evaluate the following:

1. Whether or not this individual is impaired
2. The degree of that impairment
3. The appropriateness of intervention
4. Who should be involved in intervention
5. Who else in the family system may have a similar problem
6. Who would be likely to sabotage the intervention

The trained professional usually can get a grasp of these items in an initial one-hour interview. Based upon the data you are able to provide, he or she can begin to properly advise you on what approach to take and how to involve others who care for the chemically dependent person.

As a result of your having sought professional help and educated yourself about the problem, you need to be mindful of the fact that you may be far ahead of other members of the family system and others who are close to the chemically dependent individual. You have begun to understand that intervention does not have to mean confrontation and that it is not as frightening and scary as it first sounds. But you should also know that others may be lagging behind you. Your interventionist should guide you in your efforts to get others involved.

I encourage the person who is initiating the intervention process not to ask other people — family, friends, employer — to make a commitment to "intervention," but simply to be willing to come with you to get some education and to decide for themselves whether or not they wish to be involved. If from the outset you ask them to commit to intervention, it is going to bring out their fear of confrontation, and they may either refuse to get involved or withdraw; by asking people in this way, you increase the likelihood that they will sabotage the process.

Once you have discussed these items in the first session with your interventionist, you should be ready to contact others and to request them to become involved in the scheduling of the second meeting.

The Second Step: Meeting

At the second meeting with your interventionist are people who are important to the alcoholic or chemically dependent person: parents, children, friends, pastor, physician, employer. They are all there for the same reason: each person cares about the well-being of the chemically dependent person. Each may have varying degrees of knowledge of the individual's impairment; the important factor is that they care. This session with the interventionist is designed in large part to provide this expanded group with information upon which they can base a decision. They need to learn that they are dealing with a disease and that, barring intervention, the disease will progress. If they can reach an understanding that it is indeed a disease and that the individual does not have the wherewithal to deal with it alone, then not only will they feel free to participate in the intervention, but they will quickly be able to see that it is the only common-sense thing to do.

Once the education session is completed, each individual makes a personal decision about participating. Then a group consensus about the intervention is developed, and step three of the intervention prcoess begins.

The Third Step: Preparation, Rehearsal, Intervention

No one aspect of the intervention process can be viewed as more important than the other. Each is a building block. For the group to be able to prepare without fear, the two previous steps must have been completed.

During the intervention we ask each individual to begin by making a firm statement of why they are participating, such as "John or Mary, I am here today because I care about you," or "I am here today because I love you."

In preparing the specific scripts to be utilized in the intervention, careful consideration is given to the defense mechanisms and the belief system of the chemically dependent person. As you will recall, part of the belief system of the chemically dependent person is that no one really does care and no one really does understand. To help neutralize that faulty belief system, each individual carefully prepares every word that will be said at the intervention.

To that end, we ask the members of the group to expound on why they care. We ask that they each share a brief paragraph or two about what is special about the chemically dependent person, what's good and decent about that person, what endears him or her to them. By anchoring the intervention process in love and in the B side of the personality structure of the chemically dependent person, we are able to move far away from confrontation. Throughout this preparation process the professionally trained interventionist is present to help the participants find wording that will be effective and nonthreatening.

For example, a 17-year-old son might phrase this particular aspect of the intervention this way:

> Dad, there have been times when I have felt especially close to you. I don't know whether it was because I am your oldest son, but there are many times when I have felt like my relationship with you has been special.

I remember feeling so proud when you coached my T-ball team. I remember the pine-box derby, which was a father-and-son project, and even though the car we made didn't have a chance at winning, and might even have been a little ugly, we did it together. And you really made me feel included and special.

Notice the absence of anger, the absence of blame, and the presence of love. The first two key components of the intervention process are now present. One is the love. The other is the supporting data of that love. Simply stating that you love somebody (without the supporting data) will not be heard by the alcoholic or chemically dependent person. Their defense mechanisms have evolved to the point that those words by themselves lack believability. Details need to be provided. For family members and those close to the chemically dependent person to communicate love and to share supporting details and feelings, they will need to have received enough assistance to get past their own anger.

Now that these two important components, the love and the supporting evidence of that love, are in place, participants can share concerns. The concerns that they will share with their alcoholic or chemically dependent loved one are examples of specific symptoms of the disease. If we can talk about the symptoms of the disease rather than about bad behavior or screw-ups by the individual, then we can frame things in a hearable way. Because the natural defense mechanisms of impaired individuals include the ability to be able to excuse, rationalize and justify events surrounding their disease, this particular piece of the intervention preparation is designed to neutralize and get past those defense mechanisms.

It is important to share with impaired individuals the facts of their impairment and their specific symptoms:

What happened?
When did it happen?

What were the resulting effects of the situation upon you
and the rest of the family system?

To help understand the preparation for this part of the intervention process, let us use as an example the same young man we cited previously. This young adult was a junior in high school and had been excelling in basketball. However, he had decided in his junior year that basically he was only playing basketball in hopes of solidifying his relationship with his father and that it was really not fun for him anymore. At the beginning of his junior year he decided not to go out for basketball. Here is how he shared his recollection of that event and how he portrayed his father's symptoms of alcoholism:

> Dad, as much as I care, I am equally concerned. Do you remember last fall when I told you I did not want to go out for basketball? You became very angry and quickly began calling me all sorts of names, including being a quitter, a sissy, a wimp, and many other names that are too painful to mention. Not only did your angry words get out of control but you began throwing me around and hitting me. You had been drinking that night. How much I don't know, but enough that your speech was slurred and, fortunately, your coordination was very poor. Dad, I don't believe for a moment that what occurred that night would have occurred if it had not been for alcohol and your alcohol problem. Sober, you would never act that way or ever intentionally try to physically harm me.

Take notice of what was shared:

> It is nonjudgmental in nature.
> It is caring but it points out the symptoms of the disease:
>   its effects upon the alcoholic
>   its effects upon his son

Not only is an intervention being done on the alcoholic, but also on the dysfunctional family system and on the secrets of that system. The son in this case has progressed, as a result of the preparation, to where he is able to view what is happening as symptoms of the disease and to view objectively those symptoms and their impact on himself and on his father.

A very important piece of this young man's particular statement of fact was the last sentence: "Dad, I know this wouldn't have happened if you hadn't been drinking." What this sentence says is, "I love you and I care about you. Apart from the disease, you are OK. It is the disease I am confronting and it is you who I am loving and supporting."

Each member of the family system who experienced that particular event that evening was affected by the surfacing of the symptoms of the disease, but each was affected individually and differently from this young man. The effects upon a small child are far different from the effects on a 17-year-old.

Frequently in interventions different family members don't want to talk about the same event because they feel someone else has already done so. But what is important about the event is each individual's perceptions of it and its impact on each of them.

Let's take this same situation in the same family and view it through the eyes of the spouse. She verbalized her concerns about that same evening this way:

> Honey, Brad has shared with you about the night when he told you he wanted to quit basketball. I would like to share with you some things you don't know about that night that occurred only because of the drinking. After you were done fighting with Brad, you left and squealed the tires of the car on the way out. I did not see you again until early morning. Brad also left and I did not hear from him for several hours.
>
> The fear that I lived with until I heard from Brad was immense. I did not know whether or not he was OK, whether he was so hurt he would do harm to himself, or whether he had been in an accident.

He finally called me four hours later. He was OK and at a friend's. I felt a tremendous sense of relief just knowing he was OK, but I had no idea about your safety. Did you get in a car accident? Did you get arrested for drunk driving? If you did get in an accident, were you hurt? Was someone else hurt?

I could see the fear in our daughter's face [the daughter is eight years old]. I paced the floor. I worried. I tried to act brave and tried to pretend that everything was fine. I know that intentionally you would not want any of that evening to have occurred or to ever have it reoccur. But John, when you drink your personality changes and your actions become unpredictable. You are not the problem. But alcohol is a problem.

Take special notice again of the fact that this statement encompasses the essential components that are necessary for successful intervention. It is loving. It is gentle. It is specific in the way it demonstrates the symptoms of the disease of alcoholism. And most of all, it points out that alcohol, not the individual, is the villain.

Keep uppermost in your mind that the goal of careful preparation is to neutralize the belief system of the alcoholic and to bypass the defense mechanisms this disease creates, so that recovery can begin. Since this is such a critical aspect, let's review again the belief system we are trying to neutralize and the defense mechanisms we are trying to bypass. The belief system of the alcoholic follows:

1. I know I have a problem, but . . . .
2. Nobody would understand.
3. Nobody would accept me.
4. I am different, I am unique.

It is this belief system that triggers the defense mechanisms of denial. These dominant defense mechanisms surface:

1. Rationalization
2. Justification
3. Minimization
4. Blaming
5. Excusing
6. Making alibis
7. Anger

The participants' statements above serve very well to neutralize the belief system and bypass the defense mechanism. The manner and the style in which they are written and presented give a message to the alcoholic of understanding and caring. Anger will bring an angry response. Blaming will bring blaming. Excusing or justifying will bring excusing or justifying. The statements cited have none of these problems.

As the preparation and rehearsal process continues, each participant's script for the intervention is carefully checked by the trained interventionist in order to eliminate words or phrases that are going to hook the alcoholic's defense mechanisms in a way that would be destructive to the intervention process. Words and phrases like "I think," "kind of," "sort of," "maybe" — all of these tend to rescue and enable the individual.

Once everyone's data sheet has been reviewed by the interventionist, participants are ready for rehearsal.

The Rehearsal. The goals and objectives that are to be accomplished in rehearsing the actual intervention are twofold:

To help family and friends feel the sense of power
   that they have collectively
To help participants to get an idea of how the alcholic
   will respond and to help them grasp the potential
   for success

The interventionist will have given considerable thought to the seating arrangements for the intervention. He will have thought out carefully who will be sitting next to the alcoholic and in what order people will be presenting their data. Also, the interventionist may have somebody sitting in the alcoholic's chair to help enhance the realness of the rehearsal. The interventionist will be watching for difficulties that may surface which would be disruptive to the intervention process. He will be observing particularly whose anger is getting hooked, who wants to start ad-libbing. He will be watching for the fear level that exists among the participants and providing whatever reassurance is necessary to help make participation in the actual intervention possible. If one of the participants does begin getting into his or her anger, it simply means that more work with that individual is needed. I define anger as stuffed hurt and stuffed fear. By continuing to work with those individuals who are angry, we will be able to get past that anger and help them communicate the hurt and the fear they are feeling.

After the rehearsal has been completed, participants are asked to share their opinions on how successful they perceive the process to be. If this rehearsal had been the actual intervention, what would the chances have been that the individual would have entered treatment — 10%? 50%? 90%? In other words, what is the level of optimism among the participants? Typically what happens is that a group of individuals who used to feel hopeless will now feel empowered; they will be extremely optimistic that they can make a difference and that they are going to be successful in reaching the one they care about.

Once the group of significant others feels this sense of empowerment, they are ready to face the question of where to do the intervention and how to get the chemically dependent person to the intervention. I am not and have never been an advocate of doing the intervention on the alcoholic's turf, whether that be in their home or in their office. Whenever possible, I want the intervention to be done in the interventionist's office. If we look at the history of intervention, often the alcoholic was lied to in order to get him to the meeting, or people simply walked in and surprised him. If at all possible, I want to avoid that, simply because it hooks the defense mechanisms and gives the chemically dependent person an opportunity to make excuses and to rationalize the whole thing because he or she was lied to.

Whenever a family member comes to me to initiate the intervention process, after the first session I ask that individual to share with his loved one that he has seen a therapist and is going to continue to do so, and that at some point in time others are going to be asked to come also. The only time that I do not do it that way is when there is a threat of violence or a risk of such a statement causing the loved one to run. This announcement needs to be shared with the alcoholic when he is sober, not when he has been drinking. It is not something to be debated or argued about, but simply a factual statement to be made.

If the alcoholic gets defensive when he or she is told that a loved one is seeking help, the individual is simply instructed to say that he was asked not to argue about it or discuss it, but simply to inform. This accomplishes a couple of positive things. First, the family member no longer feels the need to sneak around in secrecy to meetings with the interventionist. And second, it gives the chemically dependent person an opportunity to give some careful thought to his disease. Secretly he knows that the concern is about the alcoholism and that at some point in time he is going to have to face it.

Often this announcement will bring about a change in the drinking pattern and subsequent behavior, providing an opportunity for the family to prepare for intervention in a less tense manner. However, don't let that temporary change delude you into believing that things are better now. Remember that we are dealing with a disease that is progressive and has a very predictable and definable course. An interruption of that course is only temporary, and you can fully trust the disease to resurface and to continue on the downward spiral.

The alcoholic is not necessarily told that the meeting he is asked to come to is about him and about his alcoholism, but he at least knows that he is coming to see a therapist. Because part of his belief system is that he knows alcohol is a problem for him, he fully anticipates and expects that the problem will be raised. If, after careful consideration and planning, the consensus of the group participating in the intervention is that the individual who started this process is not the best person to get the alcoholic to the intervention, then other plans and strategies are developed.

Once the participants are confident that they can succeed with the intervention and that the individual asked to bring the chemically dependent person to the intervention will be successful, they are ready to schedule and proceed with the intervention. The intervention is scheduled for 9:00 a.m. and all of the participants in the intervention except the one bringing the alcoholic are asked to be there at 8:30. Having all of the participants come early allows an opportunity to review any last-minute concerns that may have arisen since the rehearsal and allows the interventionist to provide the necessary reassurance to the participants that they are doing the right thing. Before the participants arrive for the intervention, they have been asked to park their vehicles out of the alcoholic's view so that when he or she arrives there is no difficulty created before the actual intervention begins.

An Intervention. To understand how the intervention itself proceeds, it helps to look at an example in detail. We return, then, to Brad, the 17-year-old son we have already met, and his alcoholic father. Here is a description of the intervention that was prepared by his father's family and friends.

Present for this intervention is a gentleman by the name of Scott who coached Little League with John several years ago. They were very close friends at the time but have had very little contact lately. Also present are the neighbors across the street, Bryan and Martha, who have been neighbors for 20 years, as well as Brad and his 8-year-old sister, Jennifer. The spouse, Karen, will be bringing John, the alcoholic, at 9:00 a.m. Scott will be sitting next to John; Bryan will be sitting on the other side of John, with Martha seated next to Bryan. Jennifer will sit next to the interventionist on one side, and Karen will sit on the other side with Brad seated next to her. The next few minutes are devoted to answering last-minute questions of the participants, to review with them how the intervention is going to begin and proceed, and to provide whatever reassurances may be necessary for the participants, particularly the children.

At about 8:50 the interventionist asks the group to remain quiet so that the alcoholic does not hear a bunch of voices and get frightened away before the process begins. The interventionist leaves the office, closes the door, and waits in the waiting room so as to be able to greet the alcoholic immediately upon his entering the office. The plan that was devised to get the alcoholic to come to the intervention session is a success; the spouse and the alcoholic arrive promptly at 9:00.

The spouse introduces the interventionist to the alcoholic and they both shake hands with the interventionist, who takes a large, deep breath through his nose to see if he can smell any alcohol. It is extremely important that the intervention take place, if at all possible, at a time when the alcoholic has not been drinking. If the interventionist smells alcohol, he or she will more than likely say, "John, we need to reschedule our visit because one of the requirements I have is that people not be drinking when I meet with them. So let's reschedule and find another time." Though this rescheduling may be difficult for the participants, it is nevertheless essential. If the individual has been drinking, the defense mechanisms will be so pronounced that the chances of success will be extremely small.

If the individual has not been drinking, the interventionist simply guides the alcoholic and his spouse back to the intervention room where the intervention team is waiting. When the alcoholic walks into the room he is immediately shown to his chair and the process is begun as rapidly as possible. The alcoholic is in a bit of a state of shock at seeing people here that he had not expected and asks rather loudly, "What in the hell is going on here?" His friend Scott simply says, "John, please sit down." And the interventionist immediately takes over.

The interventionist begins the intervention process by explaining to the alcoholic what is happening. The interventionist opens the meeting by saying something like this:

INTERVENTIONIST: John, your family and your friends have been working with me for some time to find a way of accomplishing two very important goals for them. The first goal that they want to accomplish is to be able to share with you how much they care about you. And secondly, they want to be able to find a way to share how concerned they are. Everybody here has gone through a lot of hard work to prepare for this meeting today.

As a part of that preparation, I have asked everybody here to agree to some ground rules that I have for this type of a meeting. I want to ask you to agree to the same rules. John, everybody here has agreed not to interrupt while you are talking, and before we begin I am asking you to agree not to interrupt them. Can you do that, John?

(John reluctantly nods his head.)

John, am I to assume by the nod of your head that you have agreed not to interrupt people here just as they have agreed not to interrupt you?

(John quietly says yes.)

The only other rule I have, John, for this type of a meeting is that it is time-limited. This meeting will not go beyond an hour and a half. Everybody here has agreed to give up that amount of time to be with you and to participate in this meeting. And before we begin I would ask that you agree to be here for that amount of time also.

(John again begrudgingly acknowledges his agreement to the time rule. Once John has agreed to the ground rules, the interventionist reviews again with him how the meeting will progress and what is hoped to be accomplished.)

John, as I shared with you earlier, everyone here has worked hard at preparing for this meeting with the hopes of being able to communicate to you their love for you and their concern: concern about what they see alcohol doing to you. John, I will be calling on each person here one at a time. They will be sharing with you what they have carefully prepared and when they are all done you and I will have a chance to talk.

(The interventionist is able to see some discomfort beginning to surface in John as he squirms in his chair, but because what is occurring is being communicated in a very soft,

gentle, and nonthreatening way, John does not verbalize that discomfort. The interventionist immediately proceeds by calling on Scott. Remember that Scott is an old coaching friend whom John has spent very little time with in the last several years.)

Scott, what would you like to share with your friend John?

(Scott begins by holding his script in his hand and reading it slowly and carefully so as not to make any mistakes. He makes a lot of eye contact with his friend John.)

SCOTT: John, I am here today to be a support to you and a support to your family. I consider you to be one of the finer people I know. I recall our days together in Little League and how much I admired your talent, not only in working with kids and bringing out the best in them, but your ability to handle the disgruntled parents who felt their children had not played enough. You were able to deal with those situations without any anger, without ever belittling the parents involved. You always took time for them, you listened, and you showed that you cared about their child. Not only was it a pleasure to work with you, but it was a real pleasure to learn from you. You had a special talent in working with people, and above all you were a marvelous role model for the kids we were coaching.

You are a good person, John, and I care about you a great deal. And it is because I care that I also want to tell you that I am concerned. I am concerned about what I see happening to you and to your family. I know very little firsthand about your drinking because, for whatever reasons, you choose not to accept our invitations to dinner or for get-togethers. You have slowly withdrawn from our friendship. Even though I have not witnessed your drinking problem firsthand, I want you to know that I trust the perceptions of everybody else in this room. And because I care about you as they do I share their pain and their hurt for you and for them. I want you to hear this group of people out. Hear the love they have for you, the concern they have, and then accept the help that will be offered to you.

(Scott is now finished and the interventionist moves immediately forward to the next participant, Bryan, so as not to allow time for the defenses of the alcoholic to begin surfacing.)

INTERVENTIONIST: Bryan, what would you like to share with John?

BRYAN: John, I am here today because I care about you. We have been neighbors for nearly twenty years. We have socialized together. Our children have grown up together. We have supported each other through the difficult times of being parents as well as having shared many of the joys. For several years I have wanted to be able to reach out to you and to say something to you about your drinking. But I haven't known how.

John, about six months ago at 10:30 at night, Karen came over [Karen is John's spouse] and asked if I could come over and help you. Brad wasn't home and you were passed out in the car in the driveway and she needed some help to get you in the house. I know you don't remember it, but I do. As you partially came to you began crying at the embarrassment of having me see you like that. We got you upstairs to bed, got your shoes and let you sleep it off. I came back home without saying much to Karen.

Martha and I talked that night about how painful it must be for your wife and for your children. And how painful it must be for you. I know how much you love your family and how much they love you. Sometimes at night when you come home late and intoxicated and you and Karen get in a fight we can hear the shouting and screaming inside our house. I have wanted to come over but I don't want to interfere. And John, I am the one who called the police a few weeks ago. Things sounded so out of control that I was scared for the safety of your family. John, I know lately you have talked about leaving the family. I don't believe for a moment that that is what you want, because the only time I hear you talking that way is after you have been drinking.

Being involved in preparing for this intervention, John, I have learned about the disease of alcoholism and how much pain it causes the family, but also how much pain it causes the alcoholic. I know you must hurt very badly inside about what has been happening to you and to your family. I am asking you today to stop that hurt and that pain and to accept the treatment that will be offered you.

(The interventionist moves the process forward and calls on the 17-year-old son, Brad, next.)

BRAD: I'm here because I love you. Dad, there have been times when I have felt especially close to you. I don't know whether it was because I am your oldest son, but there are many times when I have felt like my relationship with you has been special.

I remember feeling so proud when you coached my T-ball team. I remember the pine-box derby, which was a father-and-son project, and even though the car we made didn't have a chance at winning, and might even have been a little ugly, we did it together. And you really made me feel included and special.

Dad, as much as I care, I am equally concerned. Do you remember last fall when I told you I did not want to go out for basketball? You became very angry and quickly began calling me all sorts of names, including being a quitter, a sissy, a wimp, and many other names that are too painful to mention. Not only did your angry words get out of control but you began throwing me around and hitting me. You had been drinking that night. How much I don't know, but enough that your speech was slurred and, fortunately, your coordination was very poor. Dad, I don't believe for a moment that what occurred that night would have occurred if it had not been for alcohol and your alcohol problem. Sober, you would never act that way or ever intentionally try to physically harm me.

(In addition to the above incident Brad also talks about his feelings of how he sees his Mom being treated when Dad drinks. He ends his sharing with Dad by saying something like this.)

Dad, in less than a year I am going to be going off to college. If you can accept help today we have a chance to restore our relationship before it is too late. There is still time for us to get back to being the friends we once were, but that time is short. And I don't want to waste it. Dad, please go to treatment before it is too late for us.

(Martha, the neighbor, speaks next.)

MARTHA: John, I am also here because I love you. You have been a very special friend, and you and your wife have been special confidants over the years. Rather than speak about the times when your alcohol problem has affected and hurt me, I wold like to share with you what has happened in our house as a result of this same problem.

As you know, John, our son, Bryan Jr., has had a problem with drugs. We had to place him in treatment. What I want to share with you is what the results have been and what has happened to our family as a result of his recovery. We all participated in Bryan's treatment, and as a result our family is closer today and happier today than probably it has ever been. Yes, there was a lot of heartache and a lot of pain that we had to walk through, but both he and our entire family system are on the road to recovery.

I want so much for you and your family to be able to experience the other side of this problem. John, for you, your own sake, and for your family, will you please go to treatment today?

(The spouse goes next.)

KAREN: John, I am here today because I love you. Over the years you have been my rock. And more than my husband, you have been my friend. John, everything we have worked so hard to build is slowly being destroyed by alcohol and the control it has over you.

(She shares her view of the basketball incident. As she proceeds she begins to dispel the myth the alcoholic feels that nobody knows and nobody would understand.)

John, I have tried every way I know how to help, except the right way. I've tried to cover up. I've tried to protect you. I've tried to defend you. I've lied to our friends and our neighbors and my parents about what was happening. In spite of those efforts, everybody knows that you've got a problem. My parents know. Your mother knows. Our friends, our neighbors, the school, they all know that John has a drinking problem.

Today I am choosing to stop pretending that alcohol is not a problem. I am going to get the help that I need and I am going to get the kids the help they need so that we can begin healing. John, I want you to get treatment too. If you don't, our kids are not going to want to come home from college. They will not want to bring their fiancees home. They won't want you at their wedding. And they won't want to bring our grandchildren to visit.

I dread the thought of that occurring, but I know that without treatment all of those things are possible. John, please enter treatment today for you and for us so that we can have the kind of marriage that we have had in the past, and we can be a family again.

(Jennifer, the 8-year-old daughter and the apple of her dad's eye, speaks next. She is trying hard to hold back her tears and for a moment cries openly. The interventionist gives her some support, lets her cry for a moment, helps her take a couple of slow, deep breaths, and says, "Jennifer, can you share what you have written to your Daddy?")

JENNIFER *(In a trembling and tearful voice)*: Daddy, I love you. Daddy, for my eighth birthday party I asked Mommy if I could have it after school while you were at work so I wouldn't be embarrassed in front of my friends by your drinking. Daddy, I am afraid if you don't go to treatment you're going to leave our family and I don't want us to not be a family anymore. Daddy, please go to treatment.

(Jennifer is now sobbing openly. The interventionist allows Jennifer to continue sobbing and over the tears begins speaking to John. John's eyes have also moistened.)

INTERVENTIONIST: John, your family and your friends have taken a significant risk today. They have taken the risk of sharing with you their love for you and their concern about what they see alcohol doing to you, in the hopes of being able to reach you and to give you the support and the courage you need to take that first step at accepting treatment. I know it has to have been very hard for you to sit here, not to interrupt, and to hear the pain that is in your loved ones' hearts.

Let me explain to you the kind of treatment they are asking you to receive and what it is about. John, your family is asking you to go to an inpatient treatment facility where you can learn about the disease that you have and what it is you need to do to take care of it. They have visited a number of treatment facilities, and the one they believe will work the best for you and for them is Cottonwood Treatment Center.

(The interventionist now explains to John a bit of what occurs in treatment and helps answer any questions that he may have about the treatment process.)

John, I am sure that you are concerned about work and a number of other issues. I want to share with you that your family has arranged with your employer to have whatever time off from work that is necessary until you are released from the treatment center. And your medical insurance will cover the full cost of treatment. Every possible obstacle that your family and friends were able to anticipate that may stand in the way of your beginning treatment today has been dealt with and taken care of. If, for whatever reasons, there are some they have forgotten, we will go to work on eliminating those as obstacles so that you can accept the help you need.

(John begins to speak. He first verbalizes his anger at work knowing about his situation. Then he begins to want to apologize to his family and to his friends for the embarrassment he has caused them and the embarrassment he is

now feeling. At an opportune moment the interventionist interjects.)

John, your family understands that the acts that have occurred were not willful acts. They were symptoms of the disease of alcoholism. What your family needs to hear today, far more than apologies, is action. John, will you go with your family and friends and enter treatment?

(Over the next five minutes, which to the family feels like an hour, the interventionist interacts with the alcoholic, helping to move him slowly to the point of surrender. On two or three different occasions during that period of time, the interventionist repeats the same question.)

John, will you enter treatment today?

(The interventionist is careful to make sure that John fully comprehends what it is that his family is asking him to do. They are asking him to enter an inpatient treatment facility. They are asking him to stay for the duration of that treatment, 28 to 35 days. And they are asking him to do it now, not this afternoon or tomorrow or next week, but now. The interventionist may review this with the alcoholic a couple of times to make sure there is no misunderstanding. He then again repeats his question.)

John, are you willing to enter treatment? Will you do it?

(Slowly, John nods his head. But the interventionist wants more than a nod.)

John, am I to assume by the nod of your head that you are agreeing to enter treatment? Can you say yes?

(The alcoholic verbalizes an affirmative response. The family embraces him, congratulates him, and soon they are on their way to treatment.)

The intervention that has just been described to you is not at all atypical. The time that has elapsed from when the intervention began at 9:00 a.m. until the time when the patient has agreed to enter treatment is only about 20 minutes. Even though an hour and a half was planned, often the intervention is over and the alcoholic is on his way to treatment long before that time has expired. All of the family members and friends who participated in the intervention go with the alcoholic to get him checked into treatment. They may have already had a bag packed for him prior to coming to the intervention. If not, they will bring his clothes to the treatment center later that day.

At the time of checking in to the treatment facility, the family members sign up for the family program and make their own commitment to their recovery process. If the intervention has been especially difficult, the interventionist may schedule a debriefing session for later that day or for the following day.

I would encourage you to contrast and compare this typical intervention with the original concept of intervention that was described on pages 28-32. Notice the absence of confrontation and the absence of anger, defensiveness and blame on the part of the alcoholic. The absence of confrontation allowed the intervention process to get past the defense mechanisms of the alcoholic, neutralize his belief system, and move the individual forward into treatment.

The confrontational style hooked the alcoholic's defense mechanism; it caused him to shout, to express extreme anger, and to "go nose-to-nose with his daughter until he had reduced her to tears." If the intervention process is truly intervention rather than confrontation, all of that can be prevented. If anger does surface during intervention, it will be at a far more manageable level and can be readily handled by a trained interventionist.

Because we are dealing with a disease that is chronic and progressive, the sooner you intervene the better. The sooner you intervene, the easier it will be for the alcoholic to accept treatment, and the less defensive he or she will become. And the sooner you intervene, the better the prognosis is for recovery.

5

Frequently Asked Questions

In the more than 1,000 interventions that I have done, I have seen that the fears and questions that surface in the significant others who initiate and get involved in the intervention process are frequently the same:

1. "Why is it important to have the children present during the intervention?"

Often the spouse of the alcoholic is concerned about having the children involved. Family members of an alcoholic, particularly the children, often feel that they are doing something to cause the problem. Getting them involved educates them about the disease of alcoholism and helps to bring them a sense of emotional freedom. They need to learn that what is occurring is a disease and that they do not cause diseases.

The children, whatever their ages, have been living with a lot of repressed and pent-up feelings. They need an opportunity to express their feelings and to deal with the traumatic effects that this disease has had on them. The intervention process does not expose them to anything they do not already know a great deal about. And by being able to participate, they can learn the facts rather than be burdened with what their young minds have imagined. What they imagine is always much worse than what is. In addition, unless they have been physically or sexually abused, children have the capacity to be emotionally honest, and the younger they are the freer they are to share what is in their hearts. If they are old enough to absorb and share the pain and the trauma that this disease causes, they are old enough to share the joy of the beginning stages of recovery. If one of the children has been the family scapegoat, the interventionist will keep boundaries in place to prevent scapegoating from occurring during the intervention process.

In the old style of intervention, the power came from confrontation. In this style of intervention the power comes from love. Children are able to communicate love in their own child-like but powerful way.

I remember an intervention a number of years ago in which a 5-year-old daughter participated. I allow small children to be their natural selves and to write their own scripts. In this situation Mom and Dad were separated and Mom had told her daughter that the reason they were separated was because Dad had a drinking problem and would not get help. When the daughter visited Dad she told him what Mom had said. Dad's response was, "Well, I would get some help but I'm too broke."

The daughter came to the intervention, which happened to occur on Valentine's Day. She had placed in an envelope several little candy hearts that said "I Love You," plus 26 cents of her savings. She walked over and gave Dad the envelope and said, with big tears in her eyes, "Daddy, I love you. And I know you said you could not get help because you were broke, so here is some money for you." I know of nothing more meaningful than the simple love of a child. That little girl's father not only got well but changed careers and is now a professional in the field of alcohol treatment.

With guidance, children are not only capable of handling the intervention process but are far better off emotionally for being involved in it. And if intervention fails, for whatever reasons, the education they have received will help them to understand that what is going on with their parent is not their fault, and they will know that they have tried to help. If they have not participated and the intervention fails, they will second-guess themselves and wish that they had been there. They may also believe that it is their fault that the intervention didn't work.

2. "Why can't we have just family? Won't he or she be embarrassed by having friends here?"

The answer to the latter question is simply yes, because the alcoholic already feels embarrassed secretly and privately; the intervention simply makes that embarrassment public. The goal of intervention, however, is not to embarrass the alcoholic but to help the alcoholic accept help. To be successful in doing this one needs to approach intervention differently from the manner in which every other crisis that has resulted from his disease has been approached. It has been a dysfunctional approach to try to keep alcoholism a secret.

Several years ago I had the opportunity to hear a speaker, whose name I do not recall, on dysfunctional family systems. One of the things she stated was this: If you can figure out what the rules of the dysfunctional family system are, the healthiest thing you can do for that family is to begin breaking the rules.

One of the primary rules of the alcoholic family is secrecy. If we are going to be successful, we must break the secret. The reality is that alcoholism is not a secret at all. Family and friends know that your loved one is impaired. They may not know the depth and the breadth of it, and they may not know specific details of what has been going on, but they know that there is a problem. And you will find that friends have been waiting for you to say something.

The involvement of people outside the family is important for a number of reasons:

1. It breaks the family secret.
2. There is safety and strength in numbers.
3. The alcoholic does not want to embarrass himself or herself in front of people outside the family.
4. Their presence prevents the alcoholic from blaming the spouse or the children.
5. They provide much-needed support for the family.

3. "Will I have to talk about _____?"

Frequently the alcoholic's spouse is concerned about the washing of some very private linen in public, such as impotence or an affair that the alcoholic or the spouse has had. They may not want to discuss such things in front of children or friends. Remember that the goal of intervention is not to embarrass or to shame the alcoholic into treatment, but to bathe him or her in love and reality.

Private and painful matters often do not need to be brought out in the intervention. It is extremely important, however, that you have a private session with the interventionist to discuss these things. The more the interventionist knows about the difficulties that the alcoholic is experiencing, no matter how painful they may be, the more the interventionist can help you to structure and plan the intervention to be a success. The interventionist is only as good as the data provided and cannot control or structure the intervention in a way that will be successful if you keep secrets from him or her. Rest assured that this information will be kept private.

Remember that guilt and shame are powerful deterrents to individuals accepting treatment. If the interventionist knows about those critical issues, the intervention can be structured to bypass them. When these sensitive issues are part of the disease, and when as interventionist I see that the alcoholic is refusing treatment but is unable to verbalize any concrete reason for it, I ask the family and friends to give me a few moments alone with the alcoholic and the spouse. In that private time I let the alcoholic know that I know what's been happening and that it's OK and not uncommon with alcoholism, and I say that in treatment he or she will be able to be relieved of the guilt and the shame that is felt. When the alcoholic understands that what has occurred is OK, and that help is available and that he or she won't be shamed for what has happened, a very difficult obstacle has been overcome. It is therefore critically important, even though there may be items you do not want brought out in the intervention, to make those things known to the interventionist so that he or she can structure and plan the intervention accordingly.

4. "But what if it doesn't work?"

Nothing works one hundred percent of the time. You need to keep in mind that we are dealing with a disease that causes irrational responses. Thus, it is impossible to predict the outcome of intervention with absolute certainty. However, if your intervention is properly prepared and you have the assistance of a trained professional, the chances of it being successful are over 90%, with success defined as having your loved one enter treatment.

But what if it fails? If it fails and the alcoholic refuses to accept treatment of any kind, the worst that can happen is that you will know that you have tried. You will know that you have walked the extra mile and that you have done all that you can do. You will no longer have to pretend. You will no longer have to keep a family secret, and you will become emotionally free to make healthy decisions to take good care of yourself and your children. Because your loved one has a disease that has an identifiable course of deterioration, it will provide ample opportunities for intervention at a later date or will create natural crises that will provide opportunities for the alcoholic to get a grasp of reality at another time.

Dick Selvig, who spent 30-plus years working in the field of addictions, taught me an important lesson. He said that I, as a professional, am responsible only for the message that I give and how I give it, not whether or not it is acted upon. By intervening you give a powerful message of love and hope to the alcoholic. Do not assume responsibility for whether or not it is heard. Remember that even though the alcoholic may have heard the message, he or she may not be able to act on it on the exact timetable that you wish. But the possibility of acting on the message of love and hope may still occur at a later date.

I know of no one who has participated in a failed intervention who did not feel a tremendous sense of relief for having gone through the process, in spite of the failure. Even though they were unsuccessful, they were immensely grateful for having had the opportunity to try. You, your family and the alcoholic are all worth the effort to begin recovery, whether or not that effort culminates in total success.

5. "What if I cry?"

You are dealing with subject matter that often is extremely painful, and crying is a normal, natural and healthy response to pain. Tears during the intervention process are not counterproductive; rather, they tell the alcoholic nonverbally that you care. If you didn't care, it wouldn't hurt so much. Sharing your pain gives the alcoholic permission to begin facing his or her pain also.

The family disease of addiction forces one to repress pain. Because the recovery process begins the first time you see the interventionist, it is OK to start doing things differently, to stop the repression and to begin letting the pain out.

6. "How many persons should be involved?"

There is not an absolute number. Six to eight persons is average, but who is involved is more important than how many are involved. Those close to the individual — his or her family, such as parents, spouse, children, and in-laws — should be involved if at all possible. It is equally important that people outside the family — neighbors, friends, and others whom the alcoholic respects — be involved also. Successful interventions have been done with as few as one person participating and as many as fifteen. The ideal, however, is six to eight.

The person beginning the intervention initially may find it difficult to think of others who might be willing to be involved. The only way to find out is to ask. Remember that you are asking them simply to meet with the interventionist to explore possibilities, not to make a commitment to participate in the intervention. Then they will be able to make their own decisions whether or not to be involved, based upon some knowledge of what will be occurring. Most people will respect your desire that they at least come and listen.

7. "Why do I feel disloyal, as if I am sneaking around behind the person's back?"

Although this question may not always be verbalized, I believe it is universally felt. You are feeling disloyal because members of an alcoholic family feel the need to try to keep alcoholism a family secret. The rule of not talking outside the family is often multigenerational. Remember as a child how little permission there was to talk about what was happening in your family outside the home. Not only is the family rule of secrecy strong, but also involved is your sense of guilt and shame that somehow you ought to have been able to handle this, control it and fix it on your own without outside help.

The alcoholic, in a remorseful moment, may have elicited from you a promise not to tell the kids, his or her parents, or your parents about what occurred; out of loyalty, you may have committed to that promise. You are feeling disloyal for a number of reasons:

1. You are being disloyal to the dysfunctional family rules.
2. You are being disloyal to promises that were elicited from you in a period of remorse.
3. Your own sense of self-failing is coming to the surface and you are "should-ing" yourself to death. "I should have done this. I should have done that. I should have said this. I should have said that."

Spouses and family members of alcoholics hold lifetime memberships in the "should have" club. Don't deny those feelings of disloyalty, but don't expect them to go away. Verbalize them to your interventionist, keep talking about them, and keep walking through the intervention process. If you grew up in a dysfunctional family, those feelings may be especially powerful. The more you can verbalize them, the less power they will have.

8. "How will we get the alcoholic here? What if he or she won't come?"

Tell the one you are concerned about that you are seeking help. Beyond that, one should defer dealing with this question until all of the preparation work has been done and the rehearsal has been completed. The question is far too scary to deal with at the outset and may inhibit you from following through with intervention.

If you can wait until the preparation and the rehearsal have been completed, there will be more objectivity and clarity about the situation. As a result of that clarity, objectivity, and sense of empowerment that you feel as part of the intervention team, numerous options will surface that can allow this last step to be successful. A trained interventionist can share options with you and the others involved in the intervention and assess the likelihood of success of those options.

9. "Is it normal to feel like it won't work? Is it normal to feel like it will fail?"

The answer is simply yes. Remember that you have tried numerous times and in numerous ways to get your loved one to face his or her alcoholism. It is difficult to feel that this new attempt will elicit any response different from what was elicited before. If you will follow through with the preparation process and follow the guidance of your interventionist, that feeling will slowly dissipate and be replaced with feelings of hope and optimism.

10. "Will this make the alcoholic violent?"

Unless there has been a history of violence related to alcoholism, the chances of violence occurring as a result of intervention are remote. If there has been such a history, then your interventionist will work with you to structure whatever is necessary to provide an element of safety for you and the others involved. A trained interventionist has dealt with this situation before and can advise you as to what steps should be taken before the intervention is completed. There is no reason not to proceed.

11. "Has anyone committed suicide as a result of intervention?"

In more than 1,000 interventions that I have done, suicide has never occurred, not even with persons who have verbalized suicidal thoughts. The intervention itself will not cause suicide. If there has been a strong verbalization of suicidal tendencies prior to the intervention, the interventionist will include components to help protect against it. In most states, if a person is an imminent threat to himself or to someone else, there are actions that can be taken, including mandatory hospitalization. A trained professional can help to assess this risk. Suicide is extremely unlikely.

12. "Should I try an alternative first? Is there something less intense and dramatic that I should try?"

Your interventionist can answer this question. By the time you have gotten to the interventionist's office you have usually exhausted other options. Your repeated attempts to reach the alcoholic on your own have met with failure. You have probably already talked with his or her physician, and the physician's advice about the risks of drinking have also met with failure.

Remember that this disease is a powerful one and that it is the disease that is in control, not the person. To neutralize that power takes strength, and that strength comes from communicating with your loved one, in a controlled setting, in a controlled manner, with an interventionist and others present. One of the ways you can sort out whether or not intervention is necessary is to ask yourself and, if possible, your loved one the following questions:

1. If I made an appointment for an evaluation, would he or she come?

2. If he or she did come, would the recommendations of the evaluator be accepted even if those recommendations included residential treatment?

If your loved one answers those two questions in the affirmative, then intervention is unnecessary. When you have reached the point of considering intervention, the alcoholic's response is generally not only "No!" but "Hell no!" If you are unsure what the response might be, catch the alcoholic in a sober and vulnerable moment and ask. Don't ask, however, unless you are prepared to immediately follow through with scheduling an evaluation. In most instances intervention is not only viable but the most caring choice you could make. You and your family deserve success, not another failed attempt.

13. "Do I need a professional?"

A professionally guided intervention has by far the greatest chance of success. Interventions have been done without the aid of a professional, but frequently they are very traumatic for the family. Anger gets exchanged, and although the family may be successful in getting their loved one to treatment, part of the treatment process is spent repairing the damage caused by the intervention.

An intervention without a professional should not be attempted in these instances:

> The alcoholic is beyond the early to middle stages of the disease.
> There is a hint of difficulties other than alcohol.
> Drugs other than alcohol are involved, including prescription drugs, cocaine, marijuana, amphetamines or any other illegal drugs.

There is a family history of psychiatric disease.
There have been threats of violence or actual violence.
There have been threats of suicide.

A basic rule of human relationships is that the closer one is to a situation or person, the less objective one is. One of the major purposes of a professionally guided intervention is to have an objective source and viewpoint. That guidance is invaluable to the intervention process and can help it to be nonproblematic and nontraumatic so that not so much time needs to be spent in treatment to repair the damage that the intervention caused.

To have a professional assist and guide your intervention elevates the problem to a level of seriousness that demands the alcoholic's attention and provides a sense of security and safety for the entire family. I have never had a family express to me that they wished they had done the intervention on their own. In fact, in most cases the family has expressed the belief that had it not been for professional involvement, the intervention would not have been successful.

For an intervention to be successful, all of the following must be objectively and accurately assessed:

> What stage the disease is at
> What defense mechanisms will surface
> What will hook those defense mechanisms
> What will be necessary to bypass the defense
>   mechanisms
> What data and how much data will be needed to get past
>   the denial
> What treatment will be appropriate for the level of
>   the disease

I believe this requires not only objectivity but a considerable amount of clinical expertise. If your loved one was suffering from any other disease, you would not place on yourself the burden of assessing the progression of that disease, the manner in which to interrupt that disease, and the development of a treatment plan for it. I believe it is extremely unwise for you to place that burden upon yourself for the disease of alcoholism or chemical dependency. I encourage you to relieve yourself of the burden of handling this disease alone and to seek and accept professional guidance.

Other Questions and Fears

It is impossible to answer every question you may have or to address each and every fear. Verbalize all your questions to the interventionist. There is no such thing as a dumb question. The questions you ask will help you to feel more secure, will help to create a greater degree of trust between you and the interventionist, and will help the interventionist get a better grasp of the situation so that the intervention can be structured and planned for positive results.

The same is true for your fears. Your scary feelings are not bad; they are normal and natural. You cannot do too much verbalizing of them with your interventionist. Remember that part of the intervention is breaking the unhealthy family rules that have developed with this disease. The rules of "don't trust," "don't talk" and "don't feel" need to be broken.

6

Intervention Considerations for Different Populations

Many families have come to me over the years for intervention, and each has believed that its situation is unique. Certainly to some extent this is true, but such beliefs are to a large degree a product of the family disease of alcoholism and drug addiction. And they are not at all unlike the alcoholic's or addict's feelings of uniqueness. The diseases of alcoholism and drug addiction may affect different people, but they have identifiable symptoms and a very predictable course, regardless of the position, age, or gender of those who are afflicted.

These shared characteristics allow a trained professional to predict quite accurately the outcome of intervention. In spite of the commonality, however, sometimes there are special problems. In these cases, families have special difficulties giving themselves permission to begin the intervention process and may feel quite stuck.

It is impossible in this work to cover exhaustively each and every potential situation, but I can share with you a broad enough spectrum of typical sorts of cases to help you identify with one that may be close to yours. By finding a section in this chapter that describes a situation similar to yours, you will feel a sense of hope and be reassured that you can make a difference.

In reading the following, I encourage you to focus on the similarities between these situations and your own rather than to search for the differences.

The Corporate Executive

Many families and individuals who have someone they love in a position of power and prestige — president or chief executive officer of a major corporation, for example — feel especially powerless. Part of that sense of powerlessness stems for so many from the fact that they regard this individual as superhuman. They are not able to see this individual as a human being subject to the same human frailties as you and I, especially to diseases like alcoholism and drug addiction.

One of the difficulties that presents itself with this type of intervention is that often we are dealing with an individual who has struggled to work his way up through the ranks. He or she has been a mover and a shaker and has accomplished a great deal. As a result of that hard work and personal success, families may put this individual on a pedestal and fail to acknowledge his or her humanness.

Economics are also often an issue for the family of an executive. Suppose that as a result of intervening we lose our relationship and the lifestyle to which we have become accustomed? If the intervention is handled with dignity, respect and love, you will achieve the response you desire.

The corporate executive, however, poses a few unique challenges, all of which are manageable. First, the corporate executive has peers who should be involved. That may mean some important people in important positions. Regardless of their personal or institutional importance, they respond in the same way as anyone does when he or she first hears about the possibility of intervention. They have the same fears, doubts, and anxieties but, once educated, will respond with compassion and with love.

Second, corporate executives often schedule their own calendars so heavily that often it seems impossible to make time for the intervention. This means that the intervention needs to be powerful enough that the executive feels sufficiently empowered to cancel his confidential appointments. The interventionist can help him with this.

Third, we must consider the issues of confidentiality and public relations. What do we say if we are asked? What if the press finds out? A trained interventionist, working with the public relations department of the corporation, can easily and carefully devise a plan of action for dealing with these issues. Usually, it's best just to say that the individual is unavailable. Later, the patient will have recovered sufficiently to say how he wishes to handle the situation. Confidentiality and privacy are extremely important, especially for the executive. A trained interventionist can help deal with this issue.

Certain issues that need to be dealt with will arise with every intervention. The professional's role is to help develop a strategy to keep these issues from interfering with recovery. Some issues may require much time, energy and money, but no issue is more important than the life of your loved one.

In all cases, the process is virtually the same:

> We begin with one person.
> We educate that person.
> We expand our program to include others.
> We educate the others.
> We carefully prepare and rehearse.
> We eliminate the excuses.
> We intervene.
> And we go to treatment.

If the intervention involves an executive, you may find that the only major difference is whether you go by car or by corporate jet.

The Professional Person

By professionals I mean medical doctors, dentists, priests, ministers, lawyers, accountants and psychologists. The family may place the professional on a pedestal in much the same way as they would a corporate executive. This response to the professional is most unfair and inhumane. Because most professionals are licensed, often the conspiracy of silence on the part of family and friends is far stronger than it would otherwise be. Families get caught up in the fear of the loss of the professional's right to practice, and as a result they get trapped in a web of silence and subsequent enabling.

Also, I believe we as a culture have treated our professionals very unfairly and have in many ways not allowed them to be human. Consequently, the families of professionals and the professionals themselves have a difficult time acknowledging drug or alcohol addictions. As a result, often we do not intervene until the problem becomes obvious at work.

I recall an intervention I did a number of years ago in the Midwest on a physician. He was drinking heavily each evening and frequently having blackouts. For more than three years, when the phone rang in the evening, his spouse got on the extension and recorded the name of the caller and what medical advice or prescriptions he gave. Before he went to work in the morning, she sat down at the breakfast table and reviewed with him the medical calls of the night before.

Such an enabling conspiracy of silence is not at all uncommon among families of professionals. As a result, often we do not intervene on professionals until the disease is so far advanced that treatment is difficult and the prognosis poor. By waiting, we only increase the risk to their health, to their livelihoods, and even to their patients. I have never seen a case where it was too early to intervene, only ones where it was too late, or nearly so.

Most of the professional governing boards in this country today have groups for addicted professionals. These groups have been put together to reach those who need help before disciplinary or legal action is necessary. However, too frequently the professional group hears about the problem only after it has reached crisis level and legal action has already begun. You may anonymously call the local governing board of the professional organization to which your loved one belongs and ask what services are available.

An important factor to consider with professionals is the involvement of peers. However, one of the big mistakes made with interventions on professionals is that one assumes that a professional doctor, dentist or lawyer is educated about the disease of alcoholism. Sadly, that is not true.

Alcoholism and drug addiction is our number-one health problem. Medical schools, however, still do not deal adequately with the subject. Therefore, I require physicians involved in interventions to go through exactly the same education as the rest of the participants. We prepare the same way, we bathe them in love the same way and we bathe them in reality the same way. It helps to involve the patient's professional peers, but it is not necessary.

For clergy it is most important, if possible, that a spiritual superior be involved in the intervention process along with peers. For clergy who do not have families, we involve as many brother priests in the intervention as possible. The love and the support of fellow priests is as powerful as the love and support of spouse and children.

For the most part, people in the helping professions are there because they are dedicated to helping others. Above all, they do not want to be in a position where they may be hurting others. Because of this, intervention is quite straightforward. However, although they are dedicated to helping others, they have a difficult time giving themselves permission to accept help. Once that hurdle is crossed, we are on the road to treatment and subsequent recovery.

In addition, professionals often feel more guilt and shame than other alcoholics and addicts. That guilt and shame make it all the more important that we intervene rather than confront. Confrontation tends to reinforce guilt and shame; the patient hears "I am bad," not "I am sick."

Often because of the extent to which professional alcoholics or addicts are protected by family, office staff and peers, the disease tends to get more advanced than it does in the general population. Greater planning and preparation, however, can make intervention more effective.

The Housewife

The female alcoholic, in particular the housewife, gets trapped in the disease of alcoholism and drug addiction by cultural biases. There is a great deal of difference in our culture between "drinking like a man" and "drinking like a lady." Men with drinking problems become alcoholics. Women with drinking problems, particularly housewives, become lushes.

The symptoms of alcoholism conflict with what our culture considers to be womanly or motherly. As a result, the woman/ housewife alcoholic is quickly forced into secrecy, and most of the symptoms of their disease occur behind closed doors. The female alcoholic really believes that "No one would understand" and "No one could possibly accept me if they knew." The guilt and the shame are enormous.

The more pronounced the alcoholic's defense mechanisms, guilt, and shame, the more pronounced the family's. Nowhere is this more true than in the family of the female alcoholic. It is a perfect example of the elephant-in-the-living-room syndrome. The special problems of the female alcoholic are not with the alcoholic herself, but with her family. It is difficult for the spouse and the children to give themselves permission to go outside the family, break the family secret and talk about what is going on behind closed doors.

Often this intervention is started by a friend or one of the older children rather than by the spouse. Frequently the first step in this intervention process is to deal with the shame and denial of the spouse and the rest of the family and to give them the permission needed to proceed with intervention.

Perhaps the best example of the female alcoholic's extreme defense mechanisms is this: 90% of male alcoholics or addicts cry when they reach the decision to accept help as a result of intervention. They are able then to show at least some of their pain and other feelings. For the female alcoholic, it is the opposite: 90% go through intervention and agree to go to treatment without showing any emotion whatsoever. Intervention is just as successful, but the female alcoholic must overcome much more repression before she can be emotionally alive again.

Once the closeted female alcoholic understands that what has been happening every day is not bad and evil but part of the disease, recovery can begin and hope can be restored. That process begins by first helping the family with those same emotions and hurdles. When the husband and children understand her behavior as symptomatic of the disease rather than of a lack of love or mothering, we can be on our road to recovery.

The Adolescent

The rate of alcohol and drug abuse among young people is alarming. Statistics tell us that as many as 60% of high school kids are involved with chemicals on at least a weekly basis. The path to addiction for many of them will be short indeed. The difficulties of intervening with adolescents were perhaps best described by Mark Twain when he said, "When I was 16 my parents were the two dumbest people I had ever known, and by the time I was 21 I could not believe how much they had learned in such a short period of time."

Because of the maturational process and the struggle for independence, often parents have very little influence over the

15- or 16-year-old. Instead, influence over adolescents comes from peers, particularly old friends whom the young addict no longer sees very often.

One of the things that routinely happens with young addicts or alcoholics is that they gravitate to a peer group that uses drugs or alcohol as much as, or more than, they do. They leave old friends behind. Those life-long friends who have been abandoned need to be involved in the intervention process because they have a significant amount of positive influence. Also, there are other adults the young person respects: a coach, a favorite teacher, a youth pastor, a grandparent, aunt or uncle.

It is never too soon to intervene with the adolescent. Because the adolescent is still developing physically and psychologically it is imperative that the disease be interrupted at the earliest possible stage.

Here are some signs and symptoms of alcohol and drug problems you can watch for in young people:

1. Alcohol missing from your liquor cabinet
2. Alcohol in the liquor cabinet diluted
3. A change in peer group
4. More callers who don't leave their last names
5. Calls from kids you have never heard of before
6. A drop in grades, particularly in math and science
7. Sneaking out at night
8. Selling of records or CDs
9. Items missing from the house
10. More secrecy
11. His or her room suddenly becoming off limits
12. Hacking or coughing in the shower
13. Reddened eyes
14. Blank look
15. Erratic behavior

16. Unexplained emotional outbursts
17. Unauthorized absences from school
18. Pattern of tardiness at school

Most school counselors today have a good understanding of chemical dependency in adolescents and will be cooperative if you call them to share your concerns. Generally, someone at school has spotted the problem and will be able to work with you toward successfully helping the young person.

It is extremely rare for adolescents to be involved in alcohol and drugs without poly-addiction. Once they have begun using marijuana, other drugs quickly follow. One needs to watch carefully for the signs and symptoms of the use of methamphetamines, cocaine and the acids (such as LSD and PCP). Hallucinogenic mushrooms are also quite common in some parts of the country.

Successful interventions can be done on the adolescent without the parent having to kick or lock the adolescent out of the house, a strategy frequently suggested by tough-love groups. Chemical dependency can progress very rapidly in young people, and the more it progresses, the greater a sense of unrealistic power the adolescent feels. As a result of that power, it is not uncommon for parents and siblings to be living in fear of their family member. That is why you cannot seek help too early when an adolescent is involved.

The Professional Woman

The professional woman believes that she has climbed the ladder of corporate or professional success by playing by man's rules in a man's world. As a result, she often tries to drink like a man. Unfortunately, alcoholism progresses at a more rapid rate in women, and what seems to be a hallmark of their success can become the cause of their downfall.

It is very difficult for the woman professional to give herself permission to seek help on her own. She fears that there will be five men standing in the background saying "I told you so" and fighting to move into her position. Unfortunately, her fears are somewhat justified. That is why it is extremely important to intervene with the professional woman before it affects her job. Once her disease and its symptoms show up on the job, it is difficult indeed to marshal the support from the work site necessary to help her take the first step into treatment.

The intervention process on the professional woman needs to deal with these fears and to provide whatever safety is necessary. In addition to family and friends, it is especially helpful if a true equal of hers, one who has struggled with the same problems, can be involved in the intervention process. That person can help allay those fears even though she may not know much about the particular case. The message that her presence gives is, "I survived professionally by surviving alcoholism," rather than "I survived by denying alcoholism."

The Senior Citizen

When working with the elderly, it is of paramount importance to avoid a confrontational style. Elderly alcoholics have often been alcoholics for a long time. As a result, their adult children are often filled with anger and even rage over what is reoccurring in the third generation. If confrontation begins, where does it stop? An onslaught of information about the disease may actually trigger a total psychological collapse. If psychological collapse does not result from a harsh confrontation with the elderly alcoholic, certainly a rupture in the family fabric may occur that is worse than the one caused by alcoholism.

The intervention with the elderly alcoholic needs to take into account the individual's age and capacity to understand. Often the alcoholic's senses are clouded, and the intervention process must be adjusted accordingly. If at all possible, the treatment facility chosen for the individual needs to have staff that specialize in the geriatric alcoholic. Treatment is slower and lasts longer, but it can be extremely effective. I have had the opportunity of doing interventions on alcoholics as old as 83.

Senior citizens have tremendous respect for the professions. Therefore, including a physician and/or a pastor in the intervention is a good idea. Grandchildren can also be extremely helpful in intervening on the elderly. I know of no one who doesn't look forward to his or her years as a grandparent, having made a commitment to be a better grandparent than he or she was a parent. As a result, a special bond between grandparent and grandchild often exists, and the power of that bond expressed in love can help begin the recovery process.

These are the key components of the intervention with the elderly:

1. Gentleness
2. Respect
3. Enough information to get past denial, but not enough to destroy

One also needs to allow the elderly time for recovery. Because of their advanced age, the physical, emotional and spiritual recovery occur at a much slower pace. If that time is available, they can live out their remaining years with dignity and respect.

Often the intervention with the alcoholic is initiated by one of the adult children who has begun to see the childhood patterns they remember repeated with their children. Frequently the spouses of elderly alcoholics are so enmeshed in the disease and so co-dependent that it is extremely difficult for them to give themselves permission to take positive action. As a result, we often end up doing two interventions: one with the co-dependent spouse, followed by one with the alcoholic. A trained interventionist can help the spouse become willing to acknowledge the seriousness of the problem, to stop the cover-up, and to give permission to help resolve a problem that he or she has been living with for years.

Elderly alcoholics are also frequently on numerous medications, which they may be abusing, causing additional problems and difficulties.

The Poly-Addicted

One of the sad realities of the 1980s is that anyone under the age of 35 entering treatment today for alcohol or drug addiction is probably dual-dependent. Pure alcoholism is rapidly giving way to poly-drug abuse and poly-drug addiction. Often we are dealing with chemicals that have contrary effects on the human organism. Within a short period of time the individual can go from depression or lethargy to energy, or from a euphoric giddiness to a deep depression.

The polarizing and imbalancing effects of different chemicals and combinations of chemicals make intervention more difficult and require greater planning and skill from the interventionist. Often it is quite difficult to find a time when the individual is really drug free. The more complex the disease and the symptomatology, the more well-planned the intervention must be.

With cocaine use, one often sees great paranoia that gets in the way of the intervention process and causes the addict to perceive love as a threat. Frequently, families and loved ones become frightened by the paranoia, and this fear traps them in the disease and its web of silence instead of motivating them to seek help.

It is not uncommon for those who live with the poly-addicted to feel like they are prisoners or hostages, constantly fearing for their own safety. As a defense mechanism, many cocaine addicts threaten any family member who tries to stop them. Sometimes the addict may even threaten the lives of others.

Because the cost of street drugs can be substantial, the family must come to grips with some of the side effects of involvement with such drugs. Secondary aspects of this disease, such as drug dealing, may pose additional dangers for addicts. Also, it is quite common for cocaine addicts to be forced into prostituting themselves in exchange for drugs. That happens not only to the female addict, but also to equal numbers of male addicts.

Affected families must view these conditions as symptoms of the disease and not get caught up in emotional responses. Because the combination of mood-altering chemicals presents so many risks, one cannot intervene too soon. The addict's behavior can be complex and confusing. However, this only means that the interventionist must have greater skill and the family must prepare more thoroughly. Quite frequently, there may be drug debts to pay off in order to pave the way for treatment.

Alcohol and drug dependency continues to affect an ever larger segment of our population. However, addicts are no more likely to have simultaneous psychiatric disorders than anyone else. The difficulty lies in being able to differentiate between true psychiatric disease and the side effects of poly-drug use. A skilled interventionist and clinician will be helpful here. Sometimes, of course, the addict may also suffer from psychiatric disease. This, however, shouldn't stop intervention. Instead, the intervention must be handled with more skill and coupled with a more sophisticated treatment plan. Numerous metropolitan areas around the country have residential treatment facilities that specialize in dual-diagnosis patients.

Frequently psychiatric disease comes before chemical dependency. The individual has gotten involved with alcohol and drugs to try to relieve the psychiatric disorder. Although that self-medication may have been somewhat successful initially, the psychiatric symptoms quickly are exacerbated. The following major differences exist for intervention for the dual diagnosis:

1. A more skilled interventionist is required.
2. Longer and more detailed preparation is required.
3. Intervention takes longer.
4. Intervention is often conducted at a dual-diagnosis hospital facility.

Do not defer intervention because the individual you are concerned about may be suffering from two diseases simultaneously. In fact, because addiction can trigger the psychiatric disease to far deeper levels, steps toward intervention ought to proceed as rapidly as possible.

Intervention With Friends

Approximately 7% of the interventions that I have done did not include family at all. Frequently these interventions occur on the Lost Child of the dysfunctional family, a child who has put a great deal of emotional and geographic distance between himself and his family. As a result, the primary family has no knowledge of the alcohol and drug abuse problems. The intervention that occurs with only the friends of the individual can be equally powerful and successful.

Since we are also dealing with a family disease, it is not uncommon that the significant people in the individual's family may also have a problem. At some point, they may need to be eliminated from the intervention because of their own disease. Typically, individuals with such families are young professionals, unmarried or divorced. Coworkers and close personal friends are able to see the effects that the addict's self-destructive course has on the development of his or her career. These friends seek out an interventionist for the same reason that a family does: somebody they care about deeply is gradually destroying him- or herself.

It is important to emphasize that we are dealing with intervention, not confrontation. With confrontation the power comes from information coupled with ultimatums. In intervention, the power comes from care, concern and love. When friends care enough to risk a friendship to reach somebody and to help them help themselves, it communicates a powerful message.

Family is important but certainly not necessary to intervene successfully. If we are dealing with a Lost Child and/or a Scapegoat of a dysfunctional family, often the intervention will be more successful without family. Forcing a reconnection with a distant family may make it more difficult to accept help. Most of all, it is difficult to avoid getting involved in the family dysfunction and to prevent the Scapegoat from focusing on it. The purpose of having family involved in the intervention process is to help bathe the individual in love. If the involvement of the family does not help the individual to feel cared for, we do better to leave family out of the process and use only friends in the intervention.

The Single Parent

Because more than 50% of marriages end in divorce, many interventions are done on single parents. As a result of an addiction and a painful divorce, the single parent is often extremely frightened to seek help lest the alcoholism or drug addiction be used in a custody battle. Although the disease and preparation for intervention may be the same, frequently the single parent must face a difficult issue: "What will happen to my children while I am in treatment?"

These individuals are usually relatively young, so the risks of dual addiction are quite high. Especially when coupled with cocaine, the addiction frequently causes great paranoia. The dual-addicted, paranoid single parent may regard the request to accept treatment as a ploy to take the children away.

Such parents also may be very afraid that the noncustodial parent will try to use the addiction to gain custody. These individuals are truly in a double bind. If they do nothing to take care of their disease, they may eventually find themselves in trouble with the law. If they do nothing the disease will provide sufficient ammunition for custody fights. But if they do enter treatment, an angry former spouse may attempt to turn this positive step against them in a custody battle.

Carefully structured and planned interventions can, for the most part, lessen these risks. By working closely with the treatment facility, the single parent can often be allowed to have additional contact with his or her children. This helps allay the fear that somehow the extended family is trying to take the children away.

If it looks like custody may become an issue, it may be advisable to have legal counsel involved in the intervention process. For example, the attorney who handled the divorce and custody agreement can help advise the prospective patient of the risks and how to minimize them. Counsel can also help advise the prospective patient of the risks of doing nothing.

Do not allow potential difficulties, even major ones, to prevent you from consulting an interventionist. A skilled interventionist can help deal with the obstacles and difficulties presented by the particular circumstances of the case. Doing nothing or denying the addiction is far riskier.

A basic rule of intervention is that the more difficult it is to get an individual to accept help, the more planning must be done prior to the intervention. But if the structure of the intervention has been planned, the intervention can be just as successful as any other.

Interventions in Families With More Than One Chemically Dependent Person

Having more than one chemically dependent person in a family is not at all uncommon because we are dealing with a disease with a pronounced genetic component. Those sharing the disease may be siblings, spouses or others. This circumstance should not stop you from proceeding with the intervention.

The skilled interventionist can help you assess where to start. Frequently I prefer starting with the individual who is going to be the most likely to succeed. In doing that first intervention, we eliminate from the process other persons who are chemically dependent in order to minimize the risk of sabotage. This is especially true if we are dealing with siblings, or a child and a parent.

After you have succeeded in getting the first individual to accept treatment, your interventionist can help determine a course of action for dealing with other addicted members of the family.

Two principal courses of action are frequently followed. If possible, the second intervention may be done immediately after the first. This is almost always a good idea in the case of spouses. We will intervene first with the spouse who is going to be the easiest and most straightforward, and then immediately after with the other. If possible, we may ask the subject of the first intervention to participate in the second one. This must be done in a way that is positive and non-enabling. Frequently, participation will consist of simply saying, "This group has talked to me. I've decided that I do have a problem and I have made a decision to enter treatment. Would you please enter a companion program so that we can deal with this thing together?" If properly structured and planned by your interventionist, this strategy is almost sure to be successful.

Most treatment facilities do not allow people from the same family, whether siblings or spouses, to be in the same program at the same time. The only exception might be in a facility so large that people can be well separated during treatment. The reason for this is that family members tend to focus on the relationship and family difficulties rather than on their own recovery. However, a companion program may be found that can complement the other treatment program so that there is some joint recovery. Joint post-treatment planning is also important.

When it is not possible or advisable to do the second intervention immediately, often that intervention can occur as a part of the treatment of the primary patient. Most good treatment facilities today incorporate intensive family involvement. As a result, a second or third patient in the same family can often be very successfully intervened on as a part of the family program. Sometimes the new patient can simply take the bed of the patient completing treatment.

Multiple alcoholics and addicts in the same family simply require multiple interventions. With one particular family we did six interventions — four on adult children, one on a parent, and one on a step-parent.

Intervention on Compulsive Disorders

Other types of compulsive disorder trigger the same defense mechanisms. Whether that compulsive disorder involves gambling, work, food or sex, the behavior, defense mechanisms and personality traits that develop do not vary. Successful interventions have been done on all of these compulsive disorders and more. The success rate of these interventions is no different from that of interventions on alcoholics and drug addicts.

Intervention Following
Failed Intervention

It is not uncommon for family and friends to try to intervene without the help of a trained interventionist and fail. Because of this, these families are often reluctant to intervene again.

However, professionally guided and structured intervention can be successful in spite of a previous failure.

Although second interventions are difficult, I am frequently faced with them because of my degree of specialty. In spite of their difficulty, I often succeed. The failure of a previous intervention, with or without the help of a professional, is no reason to give up. We wouldn't give up with any other disease, and I don't believe we ought to give up with the disease of addiction, either.

7

Ending the Cycle of Co-Dependency

Co-dependents are spouses and significant others involved in a relationship with the chemically dependent. The subject of co-dependency is a broad one. At its root is how we as a society have developed and how we as extended family reinforce unhealthy caretaking behavior.

Because this book is primarily about intervention, it is not intended to be all-encompassing in its look at co-dependency. For those who wish to pursue a more exhaustive study of co-dependency, some excellent material has been written in the last few years. Anne Wilson Schaef's works, *When Society Becomes an Addict* and *Co-Dependence: Misunderstood, Mistreated* are as solid as they come, and Melody Beattie's *Codependent No More* provides a thorough understanding of the co-dependent disorder.

I call it a disorder because like the disease of addiction it has identifiable symptomatology coupled with a progressive course that ultimately renders the co-dependent as helpless as the alcoholic. If you are in a primary relationship with someone affected with the disease of chemical dependency, then you are co-dependent and at risk for developing as many difficulties and health problems as the chemically dependent person. Each day that your co-dependency goes unchecked and untreated, you lose some of your ability to relate in an emotionally healthy way and to be emotionally present in the here and now.

Co-dependents are not bad people doing bad things. Rather, they are unhealthy people caring for others in unhealthy ways. They are the loved ones of alcoholics and addicts and other dysfunctional individuals caring and caretaking for them in a way that does not work. They are beautiful people with beautiful motives whose methods do not get the job done. They are individuals with their own faulty belief systems, individuals whose own defense mechanisms get in the way of proper care and support, individuals whose own self-worth and self-esteem are lacking.

Until now this book has spoken primarily of alcoholics and addicts and their disease and dysfunction. One of the key points made earlier in this work was that because of this disease and dysfunction, the individual lacks objectivity to adequately assess and treat the disorder. This chapter is about you, the loved one of the alcoholic and addict, and because it is about you, you will naturally have difficulty being objective. Do not expect yourself to be totally objective, and give yourself permission to receive input and guidance in understanding this important aspect of yourself.

The disorder of co-dependency is not unlike that of addiction. The co-dependent develops his or her own belief system similar to that of the chemically dependent person. Let us review the belief system of the alcoholic:

1. I know there is a problem but . . . .
2. Nobody would understand.
3. No one could possibly accept me or the changes I need to make.
4. But I am different.
5. Hopelessness is coupled with denial.

The spouse or significant other of the alcoholic or addict gets caught up in that belief and denial system and begins to use the defense mechanisms of excusing, rationalizing and justifying the disorder. Compounding this belief system is the co-dependent's lack of self-worth, which causes him or her to add supporting data to the belief system. The co-dependent begins to consider whether or not he or she is at least partially responsible for the problem. The thinking goes like this:

Maybe if I'd . . .
   tried harder
   cared more
   not gotten angry
   spent money
   not spent money
   had sex
   not had sex
   been home
   not been home
   kept the kids quiet
   let the kids play
   prayed
   gone to church
   invited family
   not invited family
   been stronger
   etc., etc., etc.

Yes, there is a problem. But I should have been . . .
slicker
quicker
smarter
brighter
And if I had been, it wouldn't be that bad and
probably would have gone away. If I had been . . .
a better parent
a better child
a better lover
it probably would not have gotten out of hand.

The belief that another's chemical dependency is, at least in part, your own fault is really a false omnipotence. You do not have the power to force someone to make unhealthy choices on a daily basis. You do not and did not have the power to cause disease.

The belief that no one could possibly understand the problem and that if they did understand they would not accept it is equally powerful. This aspect of the belief system, like the first, combines the feelings and the beliefs of the alcoholic or the addict with your own erosion of self-esteem and self-worth. That combination places you in a double-bind position. First, you believe that others could not understand or accept that the one you love has a problem. Second, you believe that if others could understand or accept that there is a problem, they would be inclined to blame you for not having done more to prevent it and more to protect them.

Once we understand that all the things we as co-dependents did to try to protect and take care of the alcoholic or addict were in essence enabling behaviors, we double-bind ourselves by saying that no one could understand or accept how much we have enabled, no one could possibly accept or understand how co-dependent we have become.

The result is that we are stuck, slowly but steadily progressing to a life of more and more secrecy, more and more cover-up, more and more shame. Our denial becomes as strong as the denial of the alcoholic or addict. Our minimizing is strong, and our inability to see the elephant grows. Our senses of hopelessness and denial grow in equal proportion, and so the diseases of addiction and co-dependency grow. As the diseases grow we isolate more, and as we isolate we feel more lost, lonely, frustrated, angry and helpless. As we feel more lost we keep more and more inside, and so our self-worth and self-esteem erode. And as our self-esteem diminishes, we lose the ability to be spontaneous and emotionally present in the here and now.

We begin to live life like a rehearsal. We continually rehearse in our minds upcoming events — "If he or she does this I will respond like this." "If he or she does that I will respond like that." We daily rehearse the next potential problem, the next potential crisis, the next situation, rehearsing not one option but two or three or four to prepare for various behaviors and actions of the other person:

> Carefully calculating
> Carefully strategizing to try to control the
>   uncontrollable
> Managing the unmanageable and reasoning with
>   the irrational

To begin to end the cycle of co-dependency you must ask yourself questions that go to the roots of self-worth:

1. Am I worth a relationship with someone whose primary relationship is with me, not with alcohol or drugs (or work, gambling, food, sex)?
2. Am I worth a relationship with someone who is capable of being emotionally present on a consistent basis?
3. Am I worth a relationship in which I do not have to excuse, rationalize, justify, cover up, or keep secret someone's behavior?
4. Am I worth a relationship in which I do not have to expend my emotional energy in rehearsing?
5. Am I worth a relationship that promises more than another crisis?
6. Am I worth a relationship that is void of blame?
7. Am I worth a relationship in which I am able to care for and about rather than having to take care of?
8. Am I worth a relationship in which I do not need to walk on eggshells?
9. Am I worth a relationship in which I do not need to feel guilty?
10. Am I worth a relationship void of fear?

Ending the cycle of co-dependency does not have to do with the alcoholic or addict and his or her problem, disease and behavior. Rather, it has to do with you and your self-worth. I hope that you can discover that you are worth all of the above and much, much more. If you can, then it becomes possible for you to be a powerful force in the intervention process. If you doubt that you have a right to the things on the self-worth list, then your participation in intervention will be prone to enabling. Your interventionist can guide you over this hurdle, so don't let your doubts stop you from getting started.

Earlier in this book we discussed the belief system that evolves in the chemically dependent person as well as in the co-dependent. We also spoke of the dual personality system, or the A and B sides of the chemically dependent person. A similar tool exists with the co-dependent.

The A side (the co-dependent side) . . .

> Lets others' wants, desires and values override one's own
>
> Rationalizes and justifies each override as a special circumstance
>
> Internally promises that next time will be different, but is unable to stick to it or unable not to get talked out of it
>
> Lets opinions of others override and become more important than one's opinion of oneself
>
> Secretly blames oneself or others for the difficulties occurring as a result of alcoholism or drug addiction

The B side (the core side) . . .

> Has a strong set of goals, values and beliefs for marriage, children, etc.
>
> > When I get married I will not tolerate . . .
> > When I have children I will not tolerate . . .
> > Holidays are going to be . . .
> > I will not allow my children to be exposed to . . .
> > I will not allow myself to be treated . . .

We co-dependent or chief enabling persons generally grew up in dysfunctional families. As a result of that experience we made strong commitments to creating lives for ourselves and our families different from those we experienced. Living with addiction, however, causes a gradual but steady erosion of our commitments and beliefs.

To begin breaking the cycle of addiction and co-dependency, it is important for you to have a basic awareness of how enmeshed in the disorder you have become. As a result of that enmeshment you have moved further and further away from your true self and have become more and more co-dependent.

In our co-dependent pattern of living we develop behaviors — conscious and unconscious — that enable the alcoholic and addict to maintain a destructive pattern. Although our motives are noble, enabling behavior helps to foster and nurture the disease. The motive may be that of attempting to keep the peace and trying to prevent the problem from getting worse, but in the end the opposite occurs.

The following partial list of co-dependent and enabling behaviors will help you to get in touch with how the disease of addiction has affected you and how you have silently enabled it to continue. I have left room for you to make notes about each of your enabling behaviors.

In what ways have you protected and covered up for the chemically dependent person?

From family

From friends

From the children

From the employer

As the chief enabler of the chemically dependent person we cover up by cancelling events, apologizing for not showing up, and coming up with excuses for not being present at family functions or social engagements. When going to social engagements where there is a risk that the one we are concerned about may let his or her drinking get out of control, we work hard before we leave at trying to elicit promises in an effort to control the amount of drinking so that others will not see the difficulties. We apologize to the children and make excuses to them for the other parent's behavior, but never quite tell them the truth. We may call the employer to say that our spouse is sick.

What secrets have I promised to keep? Part of our co-dependent and enabling behavior is the keeping of secrets.

From extended family

From church groups

From neighbors

From friends

From the children

What excuses have I used to cover up? Addiction causes both the individual and the family affected with the disease to feel a great deal of shame. Frequently it is those embarrassing and shame-filled actions that cause us to keep secrets. Think of times when you or the chemically dependent person felt especially embarrassed or ashamed. Think of the secrets that you have been keeping. Write them down either in the space provided or in a separate notebook.

What beliefs and values have you slowly compromised as a result of your relationship with the alcoholic or addict? By being co-dependent slowly but steadily your own values and belief systems erode.

Historically what were your attitudes toward drunk driving, use of cocaine and marijuana, dealing of drugs? What were your attitudes toward emotional abuse of children? How have you compromised those values?

How have you compromised your religious values and your religious activities? Frequently because of embarrassment and shame about chemical dependency, co-dependents move away from their church support groups.

How have you compromised your sexual values? Spouses of alcoholic or chemically dependent persons report consistently that it is painful to attempt to make love with someone who is intoxicated. They feel used and frequently feel that they are dirty. The result is not a love relationship and shared intimacy but uncomfortable and often emotionally painful sex.

What boundaries have you set and then later backed away from? One of the things that family members of alcoholics and addicts frequently do is to set specific boundaries on behavior that results from addiction. They tell the chemically dependent person that certain things should not occur again and that if they do, they promise that they will take some specific action.

If he or she drinks and drives again, I'll . . .

If he gets drunk again, I'll . . .

If he gets stoned again, I'll . . .

If he breaks things again, I'll . . .

If the children get hurt again, I'll . . .

If the children get scared again, I'll . . .

If this happens on the holidays again, I'll . . .

What commitments have you made to yourself and/or to others that things were going to change, that the pattern of problems was going to be broken, and that you would not tolerate it any longer? (It doesn't matter whether these boundaries were shared with the other person or were simply part of your dialogue with yourself.)

It is very important for you to understand that in doing this brief inventory of your co-dependent and enabling behaviors you are not dealing with patterns that are right or wrong, good or bad. Enabling and co-dependent behaviors are a symptom of the disease. The purpose of this evaluation is simply to help you to become aware of how enmeshed and pervasive the disease has become and to develop an understanding of its effects on you and the entire family system. What has occurred are not mistakes but symptoms, not screw-ups but the pervasiveness of the disease.

Now that you have an understanding of addiction and alcoholism and how they progress, of co-dependency and how it progresses, and of loving intervention, you are ready to proceed with specific preparation for the process of intervention.

8

Choosing an Interventionist

Unfortunately there is no professional organization of interventionists and no established criteria for assessing their training.' As a result, many people who do interventions have had little or no training at all, and so the quality of their services varies considerably. I hope that this work will encourage the establishment of a national association of interventionists which can begin setting some standards for education and ongoing training. These standards will determine criteria which professional interventionists must meet to become certified.

However, until such standards are set we must deal with the current situation. Do not be afraid to ask your interventionist some very pointed questions about how many interventions he or she has done. What was the success rate? What training has he or she received in interventions? In the fields of chemical dependency and psychology?

Much of what I said about training for residential treatment staff applies to the interventionist as well. Not only must they have a solid academic background in the area of addictions, but they ought also to have some very specific psychotherapy training. The psychotherapy training will help them to have the appropriate attitude towards defense mechanisms. Defense mechanisms need to be respected and worked with rather than confronted judgmentally. Without such training, interventionists may want to rely on confrontation, and though they may be successful in getting your loved one to enter treatment, they may create as many problems as they solve.

Training in the fields of addictions and psychotherapy is only part of what is required. Interventionists must also have excellent assessment skills, since part of the task of the interventionist is to do a comprehensive assessment of the chemically dependent person and his related psychological problems without ever having seen him. This is very difficult and requires well-developed assessment skills for alcohol and drug addiction as well as for other psychological conditions.

These may seem like very high standards. I believe, however, that they ought to be minimum ones. Unfortunately, many people doing interventions today do not have this kind of training and would be unable to meet the standards that I have outlined. As a result you may have to settle for less than ideal treatment.

Here are some key questions for you to consider when selecting the interventionist who will work best for you:

1. What primary training in addiction have they received?
2. What primary training in psychotherapy have they received?
3. What primary training in intervention have they received?
4. How many interventions have they done?
5. What is their success rate?

6. What types of interventions have they done? Here are some specific categories:
   Alcohol
   Drugs
   A combination of alcohol and drugs
   Dual diagnosis
   Food addiction and other eating disorders
   Workaholism
   Co-dependency
   Gambling
7. Do they recommend families do the intervention on their own after preparation? If they do, look elsewhere.
8. Do they rely on ultimatums? If they do, they are still caught up in the confrontational style of intervention, and this indicates a lack of broad-based training.
9. Are they familiar with this book? If they have not read it, I would encourage you to insist that they do. Afterwards, sit down with them to see whether or not they will immediately adjust their style of intervention.
10. Do they receive compensation from the treatment facilities they refer to?

Asking these kinds of questions can only increase your comfort with and confidence in your interventionist. The majority of these questions do not require elaboration here because they have been addressed in some form in other parts of this book. Be sure that your interventionist does have some specific experience that matches your particular situation.

I do wish to elaborate, however, on the last two questions. Because the style of intervention I propose, which basically avoids confrontation and ultimatums, is new, the interventionist whom you choose may not be familiar with it. If he has broad-based training and has read this book, the results will be most favorable. If after reading this book he still seems to want to use confrontation or sees no reason why the family cannot do this on their own, I encourage you to find another interventionist. However, the mere fact that he has not had an opportunity to read this book ought not to disqualify him.

Whether or not the interventionist you are working with receives compensation from treatment facilities is also most important indeed. Many treatment centers around the country provide free interventions. Often the interventionist's primary responsibility is to market the treatment center; he is one of the key individuals primarily responsible for filling the treatment facility's beds. If that is his primary responsibility, then I believe he will find it difficult to be totally objective about your situation and your loved one's therapeutic needs. You need not disqualify someone merely because he is part of a treatment facility. But he should be candid about his role and flexible about which treatment facility you choose. If you are not sure, get a second opinion.

No single treatment center is ideal for every situation. Every facility has its strengths and weaknesses. How well it works depends upon the specific situation. It is most important that an interventionist who works as part of a staff and receives his compensation from a treatment facility is free to allow your loved one to enter another facility when that seems best.

There are also interventionists who may not appear to have a direct connection with a treatment facility, but who nevertheless receive compensation from a treatment facility for having referred patients. Again, this sets up a potential conflict of interest. The more removed your interventionist is from specific treatment facilities, and the more he bases referrals on patients' needs, the more objective he is likely to be.

It is my fondest hope that soon we will develop training and experience criteria that can provide the basis for a certification process for interventionists. Ethical standards must also be set to insure the interventionist's objectivity. Until these standards are enforced, however, you must be a smart consumer.

Most regions of the country have alcohol and drug resource information centers. Treatment centers in your region also can make some specific referrals based upon their experience with trained interventionists. There are also interventionists like myself who will travel far and wide to do interventions that require special expertise.

Though there is no official national organization of interventionists, I maintain a sizable file of interventionists in different regions of the country. The treatment facilities or employee-assistance program personnel in your area should have access to such a list as well.

9

Choosing a Treatment Facility

It would be most unfortunate indeed to have spent much time and money on a successful intervention only to have your loved one treated in an inappropriate or substandard facility.

Unless one has had some firsthand experience with specialized treatment for addictions, the mere mention of treatment conjures up many negative images. It is amazing to me that people still view treatment facilities as institutions that have padded rooms, restraints, and locked doors. Many also view treatment facilities as places that force the patients to drink alcohol and then force them to vomit. This so-called aversion therapy, popular in the 1950s and 1960s, has almost been eliminated from the treatment industry.

As part of the intervention process it is important that you develop confidence in the treatment facility your loved one will enter. Your interventionist often will make some very specific recommendations based on the treatment needs that he or she sees. However, you ought to visit the facility yourself so that you can overcome your fears about residential treatment.

It is also important to believe that this is the best treatment center for your situation. To help you be an informed consumer, here are some specific points to consider and questions to ask the treatment center:

1. What is the program's philosophy? Are alcoholism and drug addiction considered to be physical diseases?

In spite of all that has been written to date about the diseases of alcoholism and drug addiction, some facilities still view addiction as a symptom of an underlying psychological or psychiatric problem. This is true only in some cases of dual diagnoses. Even in such cases, however, the addiction needs to be treated as primary. Since this matter is a philosophical one, I encourage you to ask whatever questions you need to be satisfied that the program considers addiction to be a physical disease. For example, do the medical director or other staff members give lectures to their patients about the medical aspects of this disease? Does the treatment facility focus more on medical aspects of recovery or on detox? For example, do they educate patients and encourage them to change their diets and levels of physical activity?

2. How is detoxification managed?

Contrary to popular belief only a small percentage of individuals admitted to residential treatment facilities for alcohol- or drug-related problems are going to have medically serious detoxification difficulties. Since, however, the possibility of severe life-threatening withdrawal does always exist when we are dealing with alcohol and other addictions, it is most important that the detoxification staff be specially trained in the management of withdrawal and that they be under the close supervision of the medical director.

Visit the detoxification section of the treatment facility and develop comfort with and confidence in the staff.

3. Who is the medical director and what specialized training in addictions does that individual have?

A medical specialty has developed in recent years called addictionology. Many medical directors have studied this specialty. If the medical director of the treatment facility you have selected is an addictionologist, you can rest assured that his or her training in the management of addictions is first-rate. However, because it is a relatively new specialty the medical director of the treatment facility that you choose may not yet have mastered this field. That does not mean that he or she is not qualified or specially trained. Nevertheless, be a smart consumer, particularly if your interventionist feels that the patient may have a difficult detox. Ask whatever questions you need in order to feel comfortable. As a result, you will often discover medical directors who have been treated for this disease and therefore have a wealth of personal experience as well as considerable professional expertise.

4. What ancillary medical care is available if your loved one develops complications?

Many quality treatment facilities available today are free-standing facilities; that is, they are physically separate from hospitals. In itself, this poses no problem. They should, however, have an arrangement with a nearby hospital for emergency medical care should it be needed. Asking questions about emergency medical care can help to reassure you.

5. Are the 12-step programs of Alcoholics Anonymous, Cocaine Anonymous and Alanon an integral and mandatory part of the treatment process?

Community-based support groups such as Alcoholics Anonymous, Cocaine Anonymous and Alanon may evoke stereotypical images just as treatment does. You may not understand how critical it is that your loved one be involved in the 12-step programs. Rest assured, though, that such involvement is totally essential to long-term recovery.

The treatment facility ought to be doing a great deal more than paying lip service to these programs. When you look at the treatment facility's daily and weekly schedule, you ought to see a number of AA meetings held either at the facility or in the community. Transportation should be provided if the meetings are not held at the facility.

The daily schedule should also indicate patients' schedules for working through various aspects of the 12-step programs. Many top-quality treatment centers will try to move patients through the first five steps. At the very least, the patient, before leaving treatment, ought thoroughly to understand at least the first three steps. Those who do not become involved in the 12-step programs during treatment will not make them a part of their life after treatment. And those who fail to do that tend to quickly relapse.

6. Is there a clergy staff that is an integral part of the treatment team?

Earlier we spoke about the need for the treatment facilities to view alcoholism and drug addiction as physical diseases. Equally important, something must be done to remedy the spiritual depletion that occurs with addiction. Specially trained clergy can help patients to reconnect with a power greater than themselves. If specially trained clergy are not an integral part of the team, then there is a good chance that the treatment philosophy is not at all compatible with the 12-step programs.

7. What are the training and qualifications of the counseling staff?

Though this may be difficult to assess, don't be afraid to ask some pointed questions about the qualifications of the on-line counseling staff. These are the staff individuals who will spend by far the greatest amount of time with you and your loved one and so will have the greatest impact upon the addict and subsequently his or her recovery.

For a long time, the field has relied on putting recovering individuals through a six-month or one-year training program to teach them beginning counseling skills, and then putting them in charge of groups in a treatment facility. Trying to run a treatment facility staffed only by counselors with such minimal qualifications, however, is like trying to run a medical hospital staffed only by LPNs and nurse's aides.

Hopefully, the treatment facility you are visiting will have on-line counseling staff members with more training than the standard one-year program provides. More and more treatment facilities are requiring their counselors to have at least a bachelor's degree, and many have a master's degree in counseling or psychology. It also is important to find out the extent to which those without higher degrees are supervised.

8. Do the staff and the facility meet any sort of certification requirements?

Many states today require alcohol and drug counselors to go through a state certification process. National organizations may also provide certification. Maintaining certification requires continuing education. If you discover that a number of the staff have specialized certification, you can rest assured that they are probably also getting some ongoing training.

There are also accrediting bodies for the treatment facilities themselves. One of the most widely known and accepted is the Joint Commission on the Accreditation of Hospitals, known as JCAH. Accreditation by such national organizations indicates that the institution is meeting a national and widely accepted standard of care. I recall most vividly the site visits by the accreditation team during my years as a therapist in a residential treatment facility. Though these accreditation teams may be hard on the treatment staff, I have always found them to be helpful. Following each accreditation visit, I believe the quality of treatment improved. Such accreditation indicates a dedication to high standards and a commitment to quality care.

9.   To what extent are psychological evaluation and staff involvement available?

This is not only a physical disease but also a disease with many psychological and emotional side effects. Involving trained psychologists is as important as involving clergy. In many treatment facilities around the country, the psychologist and medical director are people that buzz in and buzz out of the treatment facility and are not involved in the day-to-day care of the patient. This level of involvement is insufficient.

Besides doing a detailed psychological profile and evaluation, the psychologist ought to be involved in the therapeutic planning meetings, which should occur at least once a week. You should be cautious about choosing any facility where psychologists are less involved.

10. What is the ratio of staff to patients?

Since much of the healing that occurs will take place in daily counseling groups, the ratio of staff to patients needs to be sufficiently high. If the on-line counselors conduct groups of more than eight patients, the quality of care will suffer and recovery will be more difficult. Certainly the number of patients may fluctuate, and sometimes the ratio may be exceeded for a short period of time. However, this ought to be the exception rather than the norm.

11. What is the mix of the patient population? Are different social groups represented or does the patient population tend to be homogeneous?

Professionals have debated for years the pros and cons of creating programs designed for specific populations. Such programs are highly specialized, dealing only with adolescents, women, professionals, clergy, etc.

However, adolescents are the only group that seems to have significantly different needs. For the most part, adolescents in treatment have gotten themselves in a great deal of difficulty academically, and part of the treatment involves creating an environment that supports academic activity. Also, because of their different level of emotional maturity, often adolescents have a difficult time blending in with the therapeutic groups that are an essential part of treatment.

Beyond that exception, I much prefer to see a mix of patients: men, women, gays, professionals, factory workers. The beliefs that develop as a part of this disease emphasize uniqueness and difference. "I am unique," the patient says, "I am different." Setting up special programs for particular groups encourages this unhealthy way of thinking.

This is not to say being a woman or a professional or a gay person may not involve special problems. However they can be addressed by special groups within the structured treatment process and later by post-treatment care. The instances of this disease are more similar than different, and I believe we do better not to isolate the patient or to encourage the belief in his or her uniqueness.

12. Most importantly, what program does the treatment offer for the family?

If the program for the family is less than a week long, look for another facility. Also, more and more treatment facilities are recognizing that treating the patient alone without addressing the damage caused to the family is a sure way to fail. Some years ago a professional experienced in the field of chemical dependency said that if it were up to him, he would admit the entire family. The only difference in treatment would be that the family members would not need detox. This indicates the amount of recovery required of everyone close to the chemically dependent person.

Quality treatment centers today are offering a $4^1/_2$- to 5-day intensive family treatment as a part of the treatment process for the primary patient. This must include more than education. Part of the process must involve an opportunity to address some of the damage that has occurred and to begin a recovery process for the individual family members and the family unit. It must also involve the development, with the guidance of the family therapist, of a specific treatment plan for family members' own long-term recovery.

13. After discharge, what ongoing care is provided by the facility for treatment?

The time that the patient and family spend in the intensive-treatment facility is but phase one of the treatment and recovery process. Continuing care and therapy, either at the facility or with a specially trained private addictions counselor, is immensely important. If treatment stops the day the patient is discharged, the chances of long-term success decreases. This phase of the treatment is as important as the residential phase.

14. How does the facility deal with ACOA (Adult Children of Alcoholics) and co-dependency issues?

We are dealing with a genetic disease, and in many cases with many generations of family dysfunction. It is important to address the therapeutic issues that arise from the multigenerational dysfunction. For years, experts in the chemical dependence field have believed that treatment should not deal with the issues of being an adult child of an alcoholic or a co-dependent until the patient has been in recovery for a year.

I know of no viable research that has been done to support this view. On the contrary, failing to address immediately some of the major issues adult children of alcoholics face can make staying sober next to impossible. I believe that this is especially true when these issues involve physical or sexual abuse. Much good material has been written about this over the last several years. Many victims are filled with shame that results from an abusive upbringing, and so they have been caught in a lifelong cycle of self-sabotage. Unless they can deal with these issues through intensive psychotherapy, they may well sabotage their recovery. Recovery from alcohol and drug addiction and recovery from dysfunctional families need not exclude each other.

15. Why residential treatment only?

This book addresses those situations, individuals and families for whom formal structured intervention is necessary in order to break through the denial and repression that this disease creates. If the disease has progressed so far that formal structured intervention is necessary for treatment, then all of the evidence points to the fact that residential treatment is the treatment of choice.

There are many fine outpatient treatment centers throughout the country. However, it has been my experience that if formal intervention is necessary but the individuals are instead treated on an outpatient basis, the success rate for long-term recovery is extremely low.

The alcoholic and addict has met with continued failure. Time and time again they have attempted to adjust, control, manage and treat their problems on their own. If we undertreat individuals we are setting them up for one more failure, and they may not have the emotional strength to try again. Outpatient treatment works and can be equally as successful as residential treatment. However, I have not seen outpatient treatment to be anywhere near as successful as residential treatment for patients with whom we have formally intervened.

This section on selection of a treatment center is designed to help you to be an informed consumer. However, it will not make you an expert in the evaluation of treatment facilities. Do listen to professional recommendations from your interventionist. But in addition, gather some data for yourself. Remember that the more familiar and the more comfortable you are with the treatment site selected, the more that comfort and confidence will be communicated to your loved one, resulting in an easier intervention.

10

Preparing for the Intervention

To help make the intervention process different from the confrontations of the past, it is important that preparation occur within a structured format. The following intervention preparation worksheets will help. Ample room has been left for you to make notes in the book itself if you desire. However, for privacy purposes you may wish to do your writing in a notepad.

Do not expect to be able to complete these worksheets and to be able to prepare fully for the intervention without the guidance and support of your trained interventionist. I believe that the assistance of a trained interventionist is not only important, but essential.

Worksheets

"_____, I'm here today
because I care about you.
I love you."

What is special about this person?

What behaviors and attitudes have you seen that clearly demonstrate the B side of his or her personality?

What endears him or her to you? Remember to be specific.

"But _____, I'm concerned."

"Do you remember when . . . ?"

What happened? Be specific; he or she may not remember.

When did it happen?

What did you feel?

Past event (this helps eliminate the excuse that the problems are caused by recent stress and pressure):

Recent event (this helps eliminate the excuse that it is better now, it is under control now):

Choose three other alcohol- or drug-related events that affected you and write about them.

**It is difficult to remember sometimes because
of our own denial and repression.
Here are some tips to help jog your memory.**

If this person is your spouse, what effect has his or her addiction had on your relationship?

Memory triggers:

Birthdays

Anniversaries

Communication

Sexual relationship

The children

If the person you want to help is your parent, what effect has his or her disease had on you?

Memory triggers:

Your friends

Having friends over

School events

Dates

Abuse

Blame

Out-of-control anger

What effects have you seen the disease have on your other parent?

How is that parent treated by the addicted parent?

When have you wanted to leave home because of the problem?

What effects on other siblings have you observed?

If the person you are concerned about is an adolescent:

Attitude

Grades

Old peers

Choice of new friends

Erosion of values

Long-range goals

If the person you are concerned about is a grandparent:

Effect on you

Effect on grandkids

Fear you have of future relationship with your kids

Effect on your siblings

Effect on your parents

If the person you are concerned about is a friend, what effect has the disease had on your friendship?

Memory triggers:

Your comfort level around your friend

Pain you see in his or her family

Pain you see in his or her spouse

Pain you see in his or her kids

Have you gotten involved in the addiction by protecting or covering up for your friend?

Ways you have tried to help

Do you see your friend less? If so, why?

What overall fears have you had for your friend's health and safety?

**What excuses is your chemically dependent loved one
going to use for not accepting treatment today?**

**What kinds of replies can you give
to each of these excuses?**

11

Hope for the First Time

Numerous debates were held about what the title of this book should be. One idea for the title was "Don't Let Them Die." The reason was simple. Alcohol and drug addiction kills. The book could also have been called "Don't Let America Die."

The most recent statistics available as of March 1989 estimate that one-third of America's workforce is harmfully involved with alcohol or drugs. If each suffering alcoholic and addict impacts directly the lives of at least four other people, who is left in our culture that is not directly affected by this disease?

The dimensions of the negative social impacts of addiction are enormous. For example, the economic loss in the United States as a result of lowered productivity due to addiction is estimated to be $120 billion a year. Added to this is the increased cost of health care as a direct result of this disease, and the tremendous drain which it creates upon our legal system, our jails, and our police. The health-care costs of a cocaine-addicted baby are staggering, and in some of our larger metropolitan areas a cocaine baby is born almost daily.

179

In a recent survey conducted on one Sunday in the churches in the state of Oregon, half of those interviewed said that they had somebody close to them who had an alcohol or drug problem.

I know of no sane person who is not tormented by these statistics and frightened by what is happening to our culture. Yet most of us take no action. We expect someone else to solve the problem. We pressure the schools to have alcohol and drug programs (now some schools are even doing quasi-treatment). We become angry and frustrated with our law enforcement officials for not doing a better job of stopping the flow of drugs. We become frustrated with the court system for not keeping drug dealers in jail. We hope against hope that the employer will catch the one we are concerned about and force him or her into treatment. And certainly we believe that our government ought to be doing something about it.

I submit to you that the problem of addiction cannot be solved by government, police, schools, churches or the court system. The solution has to begin within the family. You are the closest. You have the most information. And above all, you have the power of love.

It is time that we as individuals and as families stop deluding ourselves and stop hoping that someone else is going to solve the problem for us. Our failure to take action ourselves has caused what used to be a manageable problem to become an epidemic. As a result, we as a culture have been caught up in a web of denial and continue to do exactly what the alcoholic and addict does, which is to redefine what is acceptable and what is normal. I remember well the days not that many years ago when the arrest of someone for possessing or dealing a small amount of drugs made headlines in the paper. Today police are forced to look the other way unless the quantities of drugs involved are extremely large. Recently I was involved in an intervention in which the addict occasionally dealt kilos of cocaine. Law-enforcement officials were relatively uninterested in him because they had far bigger fish to fry.

Our attitudes towards drugs have changed. For example, we used to be worried when anyone used cocaine. Then we said, "Well, at least they are not free-basing." Later we said, "At least they are not injecting." Now we are on the verge of saying, "Well, it's just cocaine they're shooting up. Thank God they are not mixing it with heroin, too." We have gone from being concerned about kids in college experimenting with drugs to accepting as a normal part of life the fact that 60% of our high school students experiment with drugs. Junior high school officials accept the necessity of dealing with drugs on campus as a normal part of their day.

Not long ago I did an intervention with a young night-shift factory worker. After the completion of her treatment and her return to the work environment, she reported back to me that she and one other person were the only two people on the night shift who were not drinking or using drugs on breaks. There were over 90 people on the night shift.

It used to be that alcoholics and drug addicts tried to protect their jobs by concealing their addictions at work. Work was the last place where their symptoms would show up. But today, drinking and using mood-altering drugs at work have become routine and accepted behaviors.

At what point does the redefining of what is normal and what is acceptable stop? At what point do we as loved ones stop looking the other way and hoping someone else will act? The alcohol and drug problem in our society today is a cancer in the very fabric of our culture. It is destroying young minds. It is destroying families. It is causing a huge drain on our economy. And it is destroying lives. If our society were a patient in a hospital, the patient would be assessed as being critically ill, placed in intensive care, and probably put on life-support systems.

There are those who will read this book and say that I am an alarmist. But sometimes reality can be quite alarming. As I travel about this country doing interventions, as I have for the past ten years, I am often asked what kind of work I do. When I reply, they invariably tell me a story about someone they know and love who has an alcohol or drug problem. Never have I heard someone say, "Gee, I don't know anyone affected by that problem." I long for the day when I do.

If you are reading this book you are probably reading it because someone close to you has an alcohol or drug problem. If so, you are that person's best hope. I encourage you not to look the other way and hope that someone else will intervene. Dare to care. Care enough to try. Care enough to get professional advice. Care enough to reach out. The worst that can happen is that your loved one's addiction will continue. But with professional guidance you have an excellent chance of saving a life and making a friend forever.

If you are a loved one of someone affected with alcohol or drug problems and have gotten this far in the book, you may still be feeling afraid. Know that fear is normal and natural. Remember that it is part of your co-dependency. Equally, it is a part of our culture. We have had ingrained in us that we ought not to say things which are going to hurt people's feelings. The author John Powell perhaps says it best when he says, "The kindest thing we have to offer one another is the truth."

Yes, what lies ahead of you is scary, but I would ask you to remember that we are talking about an opportunity to save families, to save careers, and to save lives. Remember also that we are talking about intervention, which is not as traumatic as confrontation. Albert Camus, the French philosopher, once said, "We need either to walk through the fear or to succumb to it." Unless you begin acting now, the chances are that you will succumb to it. I encourage you to begin today to start walking through the fear. Go to your telephone book, find the alcohol or drug hotlines, treatment facilities, and interventionists in your community, and make that first telephone call.

From the moment you make that call, you will have started on your own course of recovery and have become part of the solution to the problem of addiction. As you continue on that journey, I wish you Godspeed.

Bibliography

Alcoholics Anonymous World Services, Inc. *Alcoholics Anonymous*. New York, 1976.

Beattie, Melody. *Codependent No More*. New York: Harper/Hazelden, 1987.

Bradshaw, John. *Bradshaw On: The Family*. Deerfield Beach, Florida: Health Communications, 1988.

Burgin, James E. *Guidebook for the Family with Alcohol Problems*. Center City, Minnesota: Hazelden, 1982.

Gold, Mark S., M.D. *800-Cocaine*. New York: Bantam Books, 1984.

Johnson Institute. *How to Use Intervention in Your Professional Practice*. Minneapolis: Johnson Institute Books, 1987.

Johnson, Vern. *I'll Quit Tomorrow*. New York: Harper & Row, 1980.

———. *Intervention*. Minneapolis: Johnson Institute Books, 1986.

Ketcham, Katherine, and Gustafson, Ginny Lyford. *Living on the Edge.* New York: Bantam Books, 1989.

McAuliffe, Robert M., Ph.D., and McAuliffe, Mary Boesen, Ph.D. *The Essentials of Chemical Dependency, Volume 1.* Minneapolis: The American Chemical Dependency Society, 1975.

———. *Essentials for the Diagnosis of Chemical Dependency, Volume 2.* Minneapolis: The American Chemical Dependency Society, 1975.

Schaef, Anne Wilson. *Co-Dependence: Misunderstood, Mistreated.* San Francisco: Harper & Row, 1986.

———. *When Society Becomes an Addict.* San Francisco: Harper & Row, 1987.

Strachan, J. George. *Alcoholism: Treatable Illness.* Center City, Minnesota: Hazelden, 1982.

Sullivan, J. Michael, Ph.D., and Evans, Katie, C.A.D.C. *Dual Diagnosis: A Guide for Counselors.* Gifford Press, 1989.

Wegscheider, Sharon. *Another Chance.* Palo Alto: Science and Behavior Books, 1981.